Cardigan Bay Guidebook

The Essential Guide to this Stunning Region from Beaches to National Parks: Explore the Coastal Towns and Wildlife

Lovelyn Hill

Copyright © 2023 Lovelyn Hill

All rights Reserved.

No part of this book may be reproduced, distributed, or transmitted in any form or by any means, including photocopying, recording, or other electronic or mechanical methods, without the prior written permission of the publisher, except in the case of brief quotations embodied in critical reviews and certain other noncommercial uses permitted by copyright law.

Dedication

I dedicate this guidebook to those captivated by the Cardigan Bay. May it be your trusted companion through your remarkable visit to the Cardigan Bay.

Table of Contents

Introduction 1
- Why Visit This Stunning Region? 3
- Geography and Climate 5
- Brief History of Cardigan Bay 7

Chapter 1 10
Planning Your Trip 10
- When to Visit 10
- How to Get There 12
- Accommodation Options 14
- Travel Tips and Safety 18

Chapter 2 22
Exploring the Coastal Towns 22
- Aberystwyth 22
- Dining and Nightlife 25
- Accommodation in Aberystwyth 26
- New Quay 29
- Cardigan 34

Chapter 3 42
Discovering the Beaches 42
- Mwnt Beach 42
- Poppit Sands: A Coastal Gem 44
- Llangrannog Beach 46

Chapter 4 50
Exploring the National Parks 50

Snowdonia National Park 50

Pembrokeshire Coast National Park 52

Chapter 5 .... **56**

Experiencing Wildlife **56**

Dolphin and Seal Watching 56

Chapter 6 .... **67**

Outdoor Adventures **67**

Hiking and Walking 67

Water Sports 71

Chapter 7 .... **78**

Cultural and Historical Attractions **78**

Castles and Historic Sites 78

Museums and Heritage Centers 83

Dining and Culinary Delights 90

Chapter 8 .... **98**

Practical Information **98**

Conclusion **111**

Highlights Recap 111

Making the Most of Your Cardigan Bay Adventure 112

Highlights Recap 113

Memories and Recommendations 114

Recommendations for Future Travelers 115

Cardigan Bay Travel Itinerary **118**

Introduction

Welcome to Cardigan Bay with this guidebook as your compass, opening the door to an enchanting world of coastal wonders, natural beauty, and cultural treasures. "Cardigan Bay Guidebook: The Essential Guide to this Stunning Region from Beaches to National Parks: Explore the Coastal Towns and Wildlife" is your key to unraveling the mysteries and magnificence of this breathtaking region.

Cardigan Bay, a gem nestled along the Welsh coastline, has earned its reputation as a haven for those seeking to escape the bustling urbanity of modern life. Its allure lies in its pristine beaches, rugged landscapes, and a diverse array of wildlife, all under the expansive Welsh skies. This guidebook stands as your trusted companion on a voyage of discovery through this captivating realm.

Cardigan Bay is not just a destination; it's an experience waiting to be embraced. This guidebook serves as a window into the heart and soul of the region, offering an authentic glimpse into its essence. From the very outset, it becomes clear that this is no ordinary travel guide. It's a comprehensive compendium of knowledge, designed to transform your journey into an unforgettable exploration of Cardigan Bay's every facet.

Embarking on a journey through this guidebook is akin to setting sail on the tranquil waters of Cardigan Bay itself. With its pages as your compass, you'll navigate through coastal towns that resonate with character, each with its own story to tell. Dive into the vivid world of marine life that calls these waters home, from playful dolphins to serene seals. Traverse the stunning beaches that stretch along the coastline, each with its unique charm and allure. Venture deep into the heart of national parks that cradle ancient forests and awe-inspiring landscapes.

As you journey through this guidebook, you'll uncover hidden treasures and secret sanctuaries. The quaint town of Aberystwyth, with its rich history and vibrant culture, awaits your exploration. New Quay, a picturesque fishing village, invites you to lose yourself in its charm. Cardigan, steeped in history and surrounded by lush countryside, beckons with its undeniable allure. These coastal towns, each a pearl on the necklace of Cardigan Bay, are waiting to be discovered.

Cardigan Bay isn't just about human history and culture; it's a sanctuary for nature enthusiasts. The region boasts two remarkable national parks – Snowdonia and Pembrokeshire Coast. Snowdonia's majestic mountains and Pembrokeshire's dramatic cliffs and pristine beaches offer a captivating tapestry of landscapes. Whether you're an avid hiker, a birdwatcher, or simply a lover of the great outdoors, these national parks have something extraordinary to offer.

One of the defining features of Cardigan Bay is its vibrant wildlife. The bay is renowned for its resident dolphin population, and seal colonies find refuge on its shores. In this guidebook, you'll uncover the best spots for dolphin and seal watching, as well as guidance on how to experience this enchanting spectacle responsibly. Birdwatchers will find themselves in paradise as they explore the diverse avian species that grace the region's skies.

As we embark on this journey together, prepare to be captivated by Cardigan Bay's natural beauty, cultural heritage, and the treasures that lie waiting to be discovered. This guidebook is your passport to an unforgettable adventure, a comprehensive resource meticulously crafted to enhance your exploration of this stunning region. So, pack your curiosity and a sense of wonder, for Cardigan Bay awaits your arrival, and the journey begins here.

Why Visit This Stunning Region?

Cardigan Bay, a gem on the Welsh coast, beckons you to explore its pristine beauty and rich natural heritage. This coastal paradise is a must-visit for those seeking an authentic experience of Wales. Here, you'll discover an array of enchanting elements that make this region truly exceptional.

The Beaches of Cardigan Bay

Cardigan Bay boasts a coastline adorned with a diverse collection of beaches, each with its unique charm. Mwnt Beach, with its secluded cove and breathtaking cliffs, offers a tranquil escape. Poppit Sands, a vast expanse of golden sand, is perfect for families. Traeth Penbryn, enveloped by lush woods, exudes a sense of serenity.

But Cardigan Bay offers more than just these well-known beaches. As you explore, you'll stumble upon hidden gems waiting to be discovered. Remote coves, secret bays, and secluded strands of sand await those who venture off the beaten path.

National Parks (Pembrokeshire Coast and Snowdonia)

Within reach of Cardigan Bay lie two of Wales' most renowned national parks: Pembrokeshire Coast National Park and Snowdonia National Park. Pembrokeshire Coast is a tapestry of rugged cliffs, pristine beaches, and quaint fishing villages. Snowdonia, on the other hand, offers majestic mountain landscapes, cascading waterfalls, and the opportunity for unforgettable hikes.

Coastal Towns (Aberystwyth, New Quay, Aberaeron, and More)

Cardigan Bay is dotted with charming coastal towns, each with its character. Aberystwyth, with its Victorian promenade and iconic pier, is a hub of culture and history. New Quay, a picturesque fishing village, is famed for its dolphin-spotting trips. Aberaeron enchants with its colorful Georgian architecture.

Wildlife in Cardigan Bay

The waters of Cardigan Bay are teeming with life. Dolphins and porpoises frolic in the waves, often visible from the shore or on guided boat tours. Seals bask on rocky outcrops, and seabirds wheel through the skies. The bay's biodiversity extends to its flora and fauna, making it a paradise for nature enthusiasts.

Exploring Cardigan Bay (Hiking, Cycling, and Boat Tours)

To truly immerse yourself in the region, explore its natural wonders by foot or bike. Numerous hiking trails crisscross the landscape, catering to all levels of fitness. Cyclists will find scenic routes winding through coastal paths and inland vistas. Boat tours offer a different perspective, allowing you to get up close to marine life and coastal features.

Geography and Climate

Geography of Cardigan Bay

Cardigan Bay, situated between the rugged mountains of Snowdonia National Park to the north and the rolling hills of Pembrokeshire Coast National Park to the south, boasts a diverse and picturesque geography. This bay spans approximately 2,500 square kilometers and is known for its stunning coastline, which stretches over 250 kilometers. It is the largest in Wales.

The bay itself is shaped like a crescent, gently curving along the coastline, with the bustling town of Aberystwyth at its northernmost point and the charming village of St. Dogmaels marking its southern end. The coastline is adorned with a series of sheltered coves, dramatic cliffs, and sandy beaches, each with its unique character and charm.

One of the defining features of Cardigan Bay is its tidal range, which can be quite remarkable. The bay experiences one of the highest tidal ranges in the world, which means that at low tide, vast stretches of sand and mudflats are exposed, creating an ever-changing landscape for both wildlife and visitors to explore.

Climate of Cardigan Bay

Cardigan Bay enjoys a maritime climate, strongly influenced by the surrounding ocean waters. This climate provides moderate temperatures year-round, making it an appealing destination regardless of the season.

Summer in Cardigan Bay, from June to August, brings pleasant warmth and long daylight hours, ideal for beachcombing, hiking, and exploring the vibrant coastal towns. Average temperatures during this period range from 15°C to 20°C (59°F to 68°F). Rainfall is relatively evenly distributed throughout the year, so be prepared for occasional showers even in the summer months.

Autumn, from September to November, offers a symphony of colors as the foliage turns golden and red. It's an excellent time for hiking and wildlife watching. Temperatures start to cool, averaging between 10°C to 15°C (50°F to 59°F).

Winter, from December to February, is a quieter season with crisp, fresh air and the occasional frost. Daylight hours are shorter, but this is the perfect time for cozying up by the fire in one of the charming coastal inns. Winter temperatures hover between 5°C to 10°C (41°F to 50°F).

Finally, spring, from March to May, sees the landscape burst into life with blossoming flowers and returning wildlife. Temperatures gradually warm up, ranging from 8°C to 13°C (46°F to 55°F). It's an ideal time for birdwatching as migratory species return to the bay.

Thus, Cardigan Bay's geography and climate provide a diverse and inviting backdrop for your exploration of this stunning region. Whether you're drawn to its pristine beaches, rugged cliffs, or charming coastal towns, you'll find something to captivate your senses throughout the year.

Brief History of Cardigan Bay

Cardigan is a region of unparalleled natural beauty and rich history. As you embark on your journey through this stunning destination, it's essential to understand the historical tapestry that has shaped the area into what it is today. Let's get into the brief history of Cardigan Bay, tracing its roots from ancient times to the present day.

The earliest evidence of human habitation in the Cardigan Bay area dates back to the Paleolithic era, with ancient cave sites like the famous Red Lady of Paviland, revealing the presence of our ancestors over 33,000 years ago. These early inhabitants relied on the abundant marine life that thrived in the bay's fertile waters, marking the beginning of Cardigan Bay's deep connection with the sea.

Moving forward to the medieval period, Cardigan Bay became a focal point for maritime trade and commerce. The town of Cardigan itself was founded in the 11th century and became a bustling port, trading goods such as wool, herring, and timber. The bay's strategic location made it a hub for seafaring activities, contributing to its economic significance in the region.

During the 17th century, Cardigan Bay witnessed its fair share of conflict. The English Civil War left its mark, with battles and sieges affecting the local population. Notably, the Parliamentarian forces captured nearby Cardigan Castle in 1645, a site that remains an architectural gem today, open for you to explore and immerse yourself in history.

Cardigan Bay's coastal towns, including Aberystwyth, Aberaeron, and New Quay, played significant roles in the region's history.

Aberystwyth, for instance, was established as a market town in the late 13th century and later became a prominent university town. It's home to the iconic Old College, which now houses the University of Wales Aberystwyth, a testament to the town's enduring legacy.

The 19th century brought a new era of change and innovation to Cardigan Bay. The advent of the railway connected the region with the rest of the country, making it more accessible to travelers and further promoting its development. The era also saw the rise of tourism, as people flocked to the coast to experience the area's natural wonders.

In more recent history, conservation efforts have played a crucial role in preserving the unique ecosystems of Cardigan Bay. The bay is renowned for its diverse marine life, including bottlenose dolphins, porpoises, and seals, making it a designated Special Area of Conservation (SAC). These efforts ensure that future generations can continue to enjoy the natural beauty and biodiversity that this region has to offer.

Today, Cardigan Bay stands as a testament to the enduring connection between land and sea, history, and natural beauty. As you explore its beaches, national parks, and coastal towns, and encounter its remarkable wildlife, remember that you are treading upon a landscape steeped in history, with tales of resilience, trade, and the timeless allure of the sea.

In conclusion, Cardigan Bay is an enchanting destination that beckons you to explore its wonders. From the moment you set foot in this stunning region, you'll be captivated by its rich history, captivating geography, and diverse climate.

The journey begins with a glimpse into the past, where ancient inhabitants roamed these shores, leaving their mark on the landscape. The medieval ports, the battles of the 17th century, and the industrial advancements of the 19th century have all shaped Cardigan Bay's vibrant history.

But it's not just the past that draws you in; it's the present and future of this region. The breathtaking beaches, the lush national parks, and the charming coastal towns all offer an array of experiences waiting to be discovered. Whether you're an adventurer seeking outdoor thrills, a nature enthusiast yearning to spot dolphins and seals, or a history buff fascinated by centuries-old castles, Cardigan Bay has something for everyone.

Its unique geography is complemented by a mild climate that makes it an attractive year-round destination. So, whether you're basking in the summer sun or exploring its rugged coastline during winter, Cardigan Bay promises an unforgettable experience.

In essence, Cardigan Bay is a timeless gem, where history, nature, and adventure converge, inviting you to embark on a journey of discovery. Come and explore this captivating region, where every moment is an opportunity to create lasting memories.

Chapter 1

Planning Your Trip

When it comes to planning your trip to Cardigan Bay, the first question that often arises is, "When is the best time to visit this picturesque region?" To make the most of your journey, it's essential to consider the timing of your visit carefully. Cardigan Bay offers a diverse range of experiences throughout the year, each with its unique charm and attractions. Let's dive into the seasonal nuances and help you decide when to embark on your Cardigan Bay adventure.

When to Visit

Cardigan Bay is a year-round destination, and the choice of when to visit largely depends on your preferences and what you hope to experience during your stay. Here, we break down the seasons to help you make an informed decision:

Spring (March to May): Spring in Cardigan Bay is a time of renewal and vibrant blossoms. The weather begins to warm up, and you'll find the landscape coming to life with colorful wildflowers. If you enjoy milder temperatures and want to witness nature awakening from its winter slumber, spring is an excellent time to visit.

During this season, coastal towns like Aberystwyth and New Quay start to buzz with energy. It's an ideal time for leisurely walks along the beach, exploring quaint villages, and spotting early-season wildlife, including seals and seabirds. The trails are less crowded, making it perfect for nature enthusiasts and photographers.

Summer (June to August): Summer is the peak tourist season in Cardigan Bay and for a good reason. The warm weather and longer daylight hours create an inviting atmosphere for beachgoers, water sports enthusiasts, and sun-seekers. The beaches, such as Mwnt Beach and Poppit Sands, come alive with families and holidaymakers.

The clear waters of Cardigan Bay beckon you for swimming, kayaking, and sailing. It's also the best time for dolphin and porpoise watching. Boat tours are in full swing, offering you the chance to witness these graceful marine creatures in their natural habitat. Coastal towns host festivals and events, making for a vibrant and exciting summer getaway.

Autumn (September to November): As summer fades into autumn, Cardigan Bay undergoes a transformation. The crowds thin out, and you'll have more space to explore its beauty at your own pace. The weather remains pleasant, with crisp mornings and golden afternoons.

This season is particularly attractive for those interested in hiking and cycling. The trails and routes are surrounded by a kaleidoscope of fall colors, and the cooler weather is perfect for outdoor activities. National parks like Snowdonia and Pembrokeshire Coast offer breathtaking vistas, and wildlife enthusiasts can still spot seals and migrating birds.

Winter (December to February): Winter in Cardigan Bay is a serene and peaceful time. The region takes on a quieter, more introspective mood. While temperatures can be chilly, it's an excellent opportunity to experience the beauty of Cardigan Bay without the crowds.

If you're a fan of dramatic landscapes and solitude, winter might be your preferred season. Bundle up for long beach walks, marvel at the rugged coastline, and enjoy cozy evenings by the fireplace. Wildlife spotting, especially seals, continues, and you'll have a chance to see them basking on the rocks.

Therefore, the best time to visit Cardigan Bay depends on your personal preferences and interests. Each season offers its unique charm, and whether you're drawn to the lively summer atmosphere, the tranquility of winter, or the vibrant colors of autumn, Cardigan Bay is ready to welcome you with its natural beauty and rich experiences. So, start planning your trip and get ready to explore this stunning region from its breathtaking beaches to its captivating national parks and charming coastal towns.

How to Get There

Getting to Cardigan Bay is the first step in your memorable journey. This region is nestled along the western coast of Wales, and while it may seem remote, reaching it is easier than you might think.

By Car

If you're traveling from within the UK, particularly from cities like Cardiff, Bristol, or London, driving to Cardigan Bay is a fantastic option. The road network is well-maintained, and the journey itself is a scenic delight. Take the M4 motorway to Swansea, and from there, follow the A487 coastal road northward.

As you make your way along this picturesque route, you'll be treated to glimpses of the stunning coastline, lush green fields, and charming villages. It's a journey that sets the tone for your Cardigan Bay adventure.

By Train

For those preferring a more leisurely approach, the train is a convenient option. The nearest major train stations to Cardigan Bay are Aberystwyth and Carmarthen. Both stations are well-connected to the rest of the UK rail network.

From Aberystwyth or Carmarthen, you can catch a bus or hire a taxi to reach your final destination within Cardigan Bay. The train journey itself offers splendid views of the Welsh countryside, adding a touch of romance to your travels.

By Bus

Cardigan Bay is served by several bus routes, making it accessible even if you don't have a car. National Express coaches operate services to Aberystwyth and other towns in the region. Once you arrive, local bus services can take you to various points of interest in Cardigan Bay.

By Air

While there isn't an airport within Cardigan Bay itself, Cardiff Airport is the nearest international airport. From Cardiff, you can rent a car, take a train, or use bus services to make your way to Cardigan Bay.

Ferry Services

For a unique and scenic approach, you can also consider taking a ferry. Ferries from Ireland, including Dublin and Rosslare, connect to ports in Wales. After arriving in Wales, you can continue your journey to Cardigan Bay by road or rail.

No matter which mode of transportation you choose, the journey to Cardigan Bay is an integral part of your experience. The anticipation builds as you draw closer to this breathtaking region.

As you plan your trip to Cardigan Bay, consider the time of year, the activities you'd like to enjoy, and the specific places you wish to explore.

Accommodation Options

One of the crucial elements of planning your trip to Cardigan Bay is finding the perfect accommodation. Cardigan Bay offers a diverse range of options to cater to various preferences and budgets. Let's explore some of the top choices.

Cozy Coastal Cottages

Imagine waking up to the soothing sounds of the ocean, with the salty breeze gently brushing against your cheeks. Coastal cottages are a quintessential choice for those seeking an authentic Cardigan Bay experience. These charming abodes can be found in various towns along the coastline, such as New Quay and Aberaeron.

Cost: Coastal cottages typically range from $100 to $300 per night, depending on size, location, and amenities.

Seaside Bed and Breakfasts

If you prefer a more personalized experience, consider staying in one of the many seaside bed and breakfasts that dot the Cardigan Bay shoreline. These family-run establishments offer warm hospitality and often serve delectable homemade breakfasts.

Cost: Expect to pay between $80 and $200 per night for a comfortable room with breakfast included.

Luxurious Beachfront Resorts

Cardigan Bay also boasts a selection of upscale beachfront resorts, perfect for those seeking indulgence and breathtaking views. Pembrokeshire Coast National Park offers some of the most luxurious options.

Cost: Prices at these resorts can vary widely, ranging from $250 to $600 or more per night, depending on the level of luxury and the time of year.

Quaint Inland Retreats

For a change of scenery, you might opt for a charming countryside retreat nestled inland. These options provide a tranquil escape from the hustle and bustle of coastal towns while still allowing easy access to Cardigan Bay's attractions.

Cost: Inland retreats generally range from $70 to $200 per night, offering a serene atmosphere at a more affordable price point.

Campgrounds and Glamping

For the adventurous souls, camping and glamping (glamorous camping) are viable options. Cardigan Bay has several campgrounds near its beautiful beaches, and you can also find glamping sites with comfortable amenities.

Cost: Camping costs can be as low as $15 per night, while glamping tends to be pricier, ranging from $80 to $250 per night, depending on the level of comfort.

Charming Guesthouses

Cardigan Bay boasts numerous guesthouses that offer a cozy and intimate atmosphere. These accommodations often come with hosts who can provide valuable local insights and recommendations, making your stay even more enjoyable.

Cost: Guesthouse rates typically range from $70 to $200 per night, making them an excellent mid-range option for travelers.

Secluded Self-Catering Cottages

If you cherish privacy and independence during your travels, consider renting a self-catering cottage. These cottages provide all the comforts of home, including kitchens where you can prepare your meals.

Cost: Self-catering cottages vary in price, with options available from $80 to $300 or more per night, depending on size, location, and amenities.

Boutique Hotels

Cardigan Bay also boasts a selection of boutique hotels that combine style and comfort. These smaller, independently owned properties often provide unique decor and personalized service.

Cost: Prices for boutique hotels in Cardigan Bay typically range from $100 to $400 per night, depending on the level of luxury and location.

Budget-Friendly Hostels

Travelers on a tighter budget will find several hostels in the coastal towns of Cardigan Bay. These budget-friendly options often offer dormitory-style accommodations or private rooms at affordable rates.

Cost: Hostel prices are generally quite reasonable, with dormitory beds starting at around $20 per night and private rooms available from $40 to $80 per night.

Historic Inns

For a touch of history and charm, consider staying in one of Cardigan Bay's historic inns. These inns often feature unique architecture and a rich heritage.

Cost: Rates for historic inns can vary, but you can typically find rooms ranging from $80 to $200 per night, depending on the inn's age and amenities.

Eco-Friendly Accommodations

Cardigan Bay is known for its commitment to sustainability and the environment. As such, you'll find eco-friendly accommodations, including eco-lodges and lodgings that prioritize green practices and conservation efforts.

Cost: Prices for eco-friendly accommodations are on par with other options, with rates ranging from $80 to $250 per night.

Quirky and Unique Stays

For those seeking a truly memorable experience, Cardigan Bay offers unique accommodation options like treehouses, yurts, and even converted lighthouses. These one-of-a-kind stays provide an unforgettable backdrop to your journey.

Cost: Prices for quirky and unique stays can vary widely, from $100 to $400 or more per night, depending on the level of novelty and luxury.

Remember to book your accommodation well in advance, especially during the peak tourist season, which typically spans from late spring to early autumn. Keep in mind that prices can fluctuate based on availability and seasonal demand, so it's advisable to secure your lodging as soon as your travel plans are finalized.

No matter your preference, budget, or travel style, Cardigan Bay has a wide range of accommodation options to suit your needs. By carefully selecting the right place to stay, you'll enhance your overall experience in this remarkable region, ensuring that every moment of your journey is as enjoyable and comfortable as possible.

Travel Tips and Safety

Exploring Cardigan Bay is an adventure waiting to happen, but like any journey, it's essential to be prepared and stay safe. Here, I'll provide you with invaluable travel tips and safety measures to ensure your visit is as enjoyable as it is secure.

Know the Tides

One of the most striking features of Cardigan Bay is its dramatic tidal range. Before hitting the beaches, it's crucial to familiarize yourself with the tide schedules. This knowledge will not only enhance your beach experience but also keep you safe from unexpected tidal surges.

Weather Awareness

The weather along the Cardigan Bay coastline can be unpredictable. Even during the summer months, it's wise to carry a light jacket and be prepared for sudden weather changes. Check the local forecast regularly and be prepared for rain or sun, often on the same day!

Wildlife Etiquette

Cardigan Bay is renowned for its diverse wildlife, from playful dolphins to majestic seals. While encountering these creatures can be awe-inspiring, it's vital to maintain a respectful distance. Do not approach or feed the wildlife, as this can disrupt their natural behaviors and endanger both them and you.

Coastal Paths and Hiking

If you plan on exploring the coastal paths and hiking trails, make sure you wear appropriate footwear, preferably sturdy hiking boots. These paths can be rugged, and the terrain uneven, so ankle support is key to prevent accidents.

Emergency Contacts

It's always a good idea to have emergency contact information handy. In case of unforeseen circumstances, you should know how to reach local authorities, medical services, and your country's embassy or consulate.

Respect the Environment

Cardigan Bay's natural beauty is a treasure worth preserving. Make an effort to leave no trace; dispose of your waste responsibly and follow any conservation guidelines you encounter during your travels.

Local Cuisine and Water

While exploring the coastal towns, indulge in the local cuisine. Try the freshly caught seafood and savor the regional specialties. As for water, tap water in Cardigan Bay is safe to drink, so carry a refillable bottle to reduce plastic waste.

Language and Culture

While English is widely spoken, Cardigan Bay has a strong Welsh cultural influence. Learning a few basic Welsh phrases can enhance your experience and show respect for the local culture.

Currency and Payment

The currency used in Cardigan Bay is the British Pound (£). Credit and debit cards are widely accepted, but it's advisable to carry some cash, especially when exploring remote areas.

Travel Insurance

Lastly, don't forget to purchase travel insurance that covers your trip to Cardigan Bay. It's a small investment that can provide peace of mind in case of any unforeseen events.

Thus, Cardigan Bay is a destination that offers endless opportunities for adventure and relaxation. By following these travel tips and safety guidelines, you can make the most of your trip while ensuring your safety and the preservation of this stunning region for generations to come.

Chapter 2

Exploring the Coastal Towns

Aberystwyth

As you embark on your journey through Cardigan Bay, one of the coastal towns that beckons you with its unique charm and rich history is Aberystwyth. Nestled between rolling hills and the sparkling waters of the bay, Aberystwyth is a captivating destination that offers a blend of natural beauty, cultural attractions, and a warm Welsh welcome.

Aberystwyth is known for its vibrant atmosphere, and there's no shortage of things to see and do here. As you explore this enchanting coastal town, you'll discover a myriad of attractions that cater to a wide range of interests.

Attractions

Aberystwyth's attractions are as diverse as they are captivating. From its historic castle to the modern vibrancy of the arts center, this coastal town offers something for every traveler. Let's delve deeper into some of the must-visit attractions that make Aberystwyth a remarkable destination.

Aberystwyth Promenade

Begin your exploration with a stroll along Aberystwyth's iconic promenade. This picturesque seaside walkway stretches along the coastline, offering stunning views of the bay and the rolling waves. It's the perfect place to enjoy a morning jog, an afternoon ice cream, or simply a peaceful moment by the sea. As you amble along, you'll encounter charming cafés, perfect for sipping a hot cup of Welsh tea while watching the world go by.

Aberystwyth Castle

For history enthusiasts, Aberystwyth Castle is a must-visit. This medieval fortress, perched on a hill overlooking the town, stands as a testament to the region's past. Explore its stone walls and towers, and take in panoramic views of the town and the bay from the castle grounds. It's a fascinating journey through time, allowing you to imagine the castle's storied past.

National Library of Wales

Just a stone's throw from the castle lies the National Library of Wales. Even if you're not an avid scholar, this institution is worth a visit for its impressive architecture and exhibitions. The library houses a vast collection of books, manuscripts, and artworks, making it a hub for Welsh culture and history. It's a place where you can immerse yourself in the rich literary heritage of Wales.

Aberystwyth Cliff Railway

For a unique perspective of Aberystwyth and its surroundings, hop aboard the Aberystwyth Cliff Railway. This funicular railway ascends Constitution Hill, offering breathtaking panoramic views of Cardigan Bay. It's a short, but exhilarating journey that provides a bird's-eye view of the town, the bay, and the lush countryside beyond.

Aberystwyth Arts Centre

Art and culture thrive in Aberystwyth, thanks in part to the Aberystwyth Arts Centre. This vibrant hub hosts an array of performances, exhibitions, and events throughout the year. Whether you're interested in theatre, visual arts, or music, you'll find something captivating to enjoy here.

Aberystwyth University

Aberystwyth is home to a renowned university, and its influence is palpable throughout the town. The campus itself is a picturesque blend of historic and modern architecture, set against the backdrop of the sea. If you have a curious mind, take a leisurely walk around the university grounds and appreciate the academic atmosphere that permeates the town.

Aberystwyth Marina

As you explore the town, don't forget to visit Aberystwyth Marina, where you can admire an array of boats and yachts bobbing in the harbor. It's a great spot for a leisurely meal, with several restaurants serving fresh seafood and local dishes. The marina's tranquil ambiance makes it an ideal place to unwind and soak in the coastal vibe.

Dining and Nightlife

Dining in Aberystwyth

Aberystwyth's dining scene is as diverse as it is delectable. When you're in town, make sure to indulge in some of these culinary delights:

Seafood Extravaganza: Given its coastal location, Aberystwyth boasts an array of seafood restaurants where you can savor fresh catches of the day. From succulent lobster and crab to delicate sea bass, you'll find an oceanic feast awaiting you. One of the local favorites is "Pier Brasserie," known for its panoramic sea views and superb seafood dishes.

Traditional Welsh Fare: To truly immerse yourself in the local culture, you must sample traditional Welsh dishes. Head to "Y Consti," a charming restaurant where you can savor classics like Cawl (a hearty Welsh soup) and Rarebit (a savory cheese dish).

International Flavors: Aberystwyth also caters to international tastes. "Medina" offers a tantalizing selection of Mediterranean dishes, while "Baravin" specializes in Spanish tapas. These restaurants are perfect if you're looking for something beyond the Welsh classics.

Nightlife in Aberystwyth

As the sun sets over Cardigan Bay, Aberystwyth comes alive with a vibrant nightlife that appeals to all tastes. Whether you're in the mood for a cozy pub, a lively nightclub, or a cultural experience, Aberystwyth delivers:

Traditional Pubs: Aberystwyth boasts a variety of traditional Welsh pubs where you can enjoy a pint of local ale or a dram of whiskey. "The Ship and Castle" and "The Glengower" are popular choices for a relaxed evening.

Live Music: For music enthusiasts, Aberystwyth offers live music venues such as "Bar 46" and "The Cambria." You can catch local bands or talented solo artists performing a range of genres from folk to rock.

The Arts Center: If you prefer a cultural night out, Aberystwyth Arts Center hosts a diverse array of events, including theater performances, concerts, and art exhibitions. It's the perfect spot to immerse yourself in the local artistic scene.

In Aberystwyth, the dining and nightlife experiences are a reflection of the town itself—warm, welcoming, and filled with surprises at every turn. As you continue your exploration of Cardigan Bay, the next coastal town on your journey is New Quay, a place where history, dolphins, and stunning coastal vistas await. Stay tuned for our in-depth guide to New Quay and all it has to offer.

Accommodation in Aberystwyth

When you're planning your trip to Cardigan Bay, one of the key aspects to consider is where to stay, and Aberystwyth offers a range of excellent accommodation options to choose from. Here, we'll delve into the various accommodation options available in Aberystwyth.

Hotels in Aberystwyth

Aberystwyth boasts a selection of hotels that cater to different budgets and preferences. Whether you're seeking a luxurious getaway or a cozy and budget-friendly stay, you're likely to find something that suits your needs.

The Marine Hotel

Situated right along the seafront, the Marine Hotel offers stunning ocean views and a convenient location for beach enthusiasts. The hotel offers elegantly furnished rooms with modern amenities to make your stay comfortable. Prices for a double room typically range from $120 to $200 per night, depending on the season.

The Belle Vue Royal Hotel

This historic hotel, overlooking Cardigan Bay, combines Victorian elegance with modern comforts. The Belle Vue Royal Hotel offers a range of room types, including sea-view options. Prices for a double room usually range from $100 to $180 per night, making it an attractive choice for those looking for quality without breaking the bank.

Bed and Breakfasts in Aberystwyth

If you prefer a more personalized and homey atmosphere, Aberystwyth has several charming bed and breakfasts to consider.

Plas Antaron Hotel and Stablau

Plas Antaron Hotel and Stablau, set in a tranquil countryside location just outside Aberystwyth, offers a cozy and welcoming stay. They offer comfortable rooms with prices ranging from $80 to $150 per night, often inclusive of a hearty Welsh breakfast.

Gwesty Cymru

For a unique bed and breakfast experience, Gwesty Cymru provides boutique-style accommodation in the heart of Aberystwyth. With a focus on Welsh hospitality, they offer a variety of room types with prices ranging from $110 to $220 per night, including a delicious Welsh breakfast.

Self-Catering Accommodation

For those who prefer a more independent stay, self-catering options in Aberystwyth are also available.

Aberystwyth Holiday Apartments

Aberystwyth Holiday Apartments offer well-furnished self-catering units, ideal for families or groups. Prices vary depending on the size and location of the apartment, but you can expect to pay around $90 to $200 per night.

Aberystwyth University Accommodation

During the summer months, Aberystwyth University opens up its student accommodations for visitors. These are basic but cost-effective options with prices starting from as low as $50 per night.

Remember that accommodation costs can fluctuate based on the time of year and special events in Aberystwyth. It's advisable to book in advance, especially during the peak summer season, to secure your preferred place to stay.

New Quay

New Quay is a picturesque coastal town nestled on the shores of Cardigan Bay. Known for its idyllic harbor and stunning seafront, this charming town is a must-visit destination within the region. As you explore New Quay, you'll discover a range of attractions that will captivate your senses and provide a glimpse into the local culture and natural wonders.

Attractions

New Quay Harbor: Begin your exploration of New Quay at its vibrant harbor. This bustling hub is the heart of the town, where colorful fishing boats sway gently in the breeze. Take a stroll along the quayside and enjoy the delightful views of the bay. You might even spot local fishermen at work, bringing in their catch of the day. It's a great place to immerse yourself in the maritime spirit of the town.

Dylan Thomas Trail: Literary enthusiasts will find New Quay a fascinating destination. Follow in the footsteps of the renowned poet Dylan Thomas, who spent some of his formative years in this town. The Dylan Thomas Trail offers you a chance to explore the places that inspired his work, including his former residence, Majoda, which is now a museum dedicated to his life and legacy.

Dolphin Spotting: Cardigan Bay is celebrated for its diverse marine life, and New Quay is one of the best places to encounter it. The waters here are home to resident bottlenose dolphins, and you can embark on a thrilling dolphin-watching boat trip from the harbor. As you cruise along the coastline, you'll likely witness these majestic creatures playfully leaping through the waves, creating lasting memories.

Pubs and Cafés: After a day of exploration, you'll undoubtedly want to savor some local cuisine. New Quay offers a range of traditional Welsh pubs and cozy cafés. Sample fresh seafood dishes or indulge in a classic Welsh rarebit. The warm hospitality of the locals adds an extra layer of charm to the dining experience.

Llangrannog Beach: While not technically in New Quay, the nearby Llangrannog Beach is a short drive away and deserves a mention. This secluded, sandy cove is perfect for a day of relaxation. The clear waters invite swimmers, and the scenic coastal path to New Quay offers breathtaking views of the rugged cliffs and sea stacks.

As you explore New Quay, you'll find that the town effortlessly combines its rich heritage with the natural wonders of Cardigan Bay. Whether you're seeking history, literary inspiration, or a close encounter with marine life, New Quay has something to offer every traveler.

Dining and Nightlife in New Quay

New Quay offers not only scenic beauty but also a delightful culinary and nightlife experience that will leave you craving for more. As you explore this picturesque town, you'll find a range of dining options to satisfy your taste buds.

The Hungry Sailor: Start your culinary adventure at The Hungry Sailor, a restaurant renowned for its seafood delights. Freshly caught fish and shellfish take center stage here, ensuring you enjoy the true flavors of the sea. Whether you opt for their succulent lobster or the classic fish and chips, you won't be disappointed. The nautical-themed décor adds to the charm, making it a must-visit spot.

The Lime Crab: Another seafood gem in New Quay, The Lime Crab, offers a relaxed dining atmosphere with a focus on sustainability. Their commitment to using locally sourced, seasonal ingredients means you get a taste of the region's best in every bite. From crab linguine to grilled mackerel, the menu is a seafood lover's paradise.

Celtic Beach Bar: If you're in the mood for a more laid-back experience, the Celtic Beach Bar is the place to be. Overlooking the beautiful New Quay Harbor, this bar offers a wide range of pub grub, making it an ideal spot for a hearty lunch or casual dinner. Don't forget to try their local ales while taking in the stunning coastal views.

Harbourmaster Hotel: For a touch of elegance, the Harbourmaster Hotel combines fine dining with a breathtaking waterfront setting. Their menu features a blend of modern British and Welsh cuisine, with dishes like slow-cooked lamb and fresh seafood. It's the perfect place for a special evening.

When the sun sets over Cardigan Bay, New Quay comes alive with a vibrant nightlife scene. Whether you prefer a quiet pint in a traditional pub or dancing the night away, there's something for everyone.

The Black Lion: This historic pub exudes character and offers a warm welcome. You can enjoy a range of local ales and live music on select evenings, making it a favorite among both locals and visitors.

Live Music Nights: New Quay often hosts live music events, particularly during the summer months. Local bands and musicians perform in various venues, adding a lively atmosphere to the town. Check out the event listings to catch a performance that suits your taste.

Starry Nights: Cardigan Bay is known for its clear night skies, perfect for stargazing. You can join guided stargazing tours or simply lay back on the beach and gaze at the constellations above.

As you explore New Quay's dining and nightlife scene, you'll find that it perfectly complements the town's coastal beauty. So, don't miss the opportunity to savor the flavors and experiences that make New Quay a memorable stop on your Cardigan Bay adventure.

Accommodation in New Quay

Bed and Breakfasts

For those looking for a comfortable and homey stay, New Quay boasts several charming bed and breakfasts that provide an authentic Welsh experience. One such option is "Trem Y Mor," a quaint B&B with a breathtaking view of the bay. Prices typically range from $80 to $120 per night, depending on the season and room type.

Holiday Cottages

If you prefer a self-catering accommodation option, holiday cottages in New Quay are a popular choice. "Ty Bach Twt" is a delightful, traditional Welsh cottage available for rent, offering the perfect blend of comfort and privacy. Prices for holiday cottages vary depending on size and location but generally start at around $100 per night.

Seaside Resorts

For a touch of luxury and panoramic sea views, you might consider staying at one of the upscale seaside resorts in New Quay. "The Cliff Hotel & Spa" is a notable choice, offering elegant rooms, spa facilities, and exceptional dining. Prices for resorts can range from $150 to $300 or more per night, depending on the season and room category.

Camping and Caravanning

For those seeking a more adventurous stay, there are also camping and caravan sites available in and around New Quay. "Cardigan Bay Camping and Caravanning Club Site" is a popular option for campers, with prices starting at around $20 per night for a pitch.

Booking Tips

1. Advance Reservations: New Quay is a sought-after destination, especially during the summer months. To secure your preferred accommodation, it's advisable to book well in advance.
2. Seasonal Variations: Prices can vary significantly depending on the time of year. Summer is the peak season, with higher rates, while you may find more affordable options during the off-peak months.
3. Amenities and Inclusions: Before booking, carefully review what each accommodation offers. Some may include breakfast, parking, or Wi-Fi, while others may charge extra for these amenities.
4. Location Matters: Consider the proximity of your accommodation to the beach, town center, and attractions. Being close to the action can enhance your overall experience.

5. Read Reviews: Take advantage of online reviews and recommendations from fellow travelers to ensure you choose an accommodation option that suits your needs and expectations.

New Quay's diverse range of accommodations ensures that every traveler can find the perfect place to rest, relax, and enjoy the stunning beauty of Cardigan Bay. Whether you opt for a cozy bed and breakfast, a charming holiday cottage, or a luxurious seaside resort, you're sure to make unforgettable memories in this enchanting coastal town.

Cardigan

The town of Cardigan is a charming starting point for your exploration of Cardigan Bay. It's not only a place of historical significance but also a vibrant hub that offers various attractions to visitors. As you wander through its streets, you'll find yourself immersed in a delightful blend of tradition and modernity.

Attractions

Cardigan Castle

Your journey in Cardigan should commence with a visit to Cardigan Castle, a symbol of the town's rich history. The castle has stood since the 12th century, witnessing centuries of stories. You can explore its well-preserved rooms, learn about its past through informative exhibits, and even enjoy a picnic on its beautiful grounds. The castle often hosts events and exhibitions, so be sure to check their schedule when you plan your visit.

Teifi Valley Railway

For a nostalgic experience, the Teifi Valley Railway is a must. This heritage railway offers a scenic ride through the picturesque Teifi Valley. As you chug along the tracks, you'll be treated to stunning views of the countryside. It's an enjoyable way to relax and take in the natural beauty of the region.

The Guildhall Market

To get a taste of local culture, head to the Guildhall Market. This bustling marketplace is brimming with stalls selling everything from fresh produce to handcrafted goods. It's an excellent place to pick up souvenirs, try some local delicacies, and interact with friendly locals.

St. Dogmaels Abbey

Just a short stroll from Cardigan, you'll find the tranquil ruins of St. Dogmaels Abbey. This ancient abbey is steeped in history and offers a serene atmosphere for reflection and photography. The nearby village of St. Dogmaels is a charming spot to explore as well.

Dining and Nightlife in Cardigan

When it comes to dining and nightlife in Cardigan, you're in for a delightful experience that perfectly complements the natural beauty and adventures the region has to offer. While Cardigan Bay is famous for its pristine beaches, national parks, and charming coastal towns, it also boasts a vibrant culinary scene and nightlife that can make your evenings just as memorable as your days. Let's delve into the delectable world of Cardigan's restaurants and cafes, providing you with a taste of what awaits you.

Exploring Cardigan's Culinary Delights

Cardigan offers a diverse range of dining options, catering to various tastes and preferences. Whether you're a seafood enthusiast, a lover of traditional Welsh cuisine, or seeking international flavors, you'll find something to satisfy your palate.

The Lion Hotel Restaurant

Situated in the heart of Cardigan, The Lion Hotel Restaurant is a culinary gem that offers a taste of both traditional Welsh dishes and modern international cuisine. The restaurant's cozy atmosphere and welcoming staff make it an ideal spot for a memorable meal. Don't miss the opportunity to savor local specialties like Cawl (a hearty Welsh soup) or try their delectable seafood options.

Crwst Café

For those in search of a casual and friendly dining experience, Crwst Café is a must-visit. This charming cafe is known for its artisanal coffee, freshly baked pastries, and light lunches. It's an excellent spot to start your day with a hearty breakfast or unwind in the afternoon with a cup of their finest brew.

Pizzatipi

Craving wood-fired pizza with a twist? Look no further than Pizzatipi, a unique eatery located in a rustic tipi on the banks of the River Teifi. Their imaginative pizzas, made from locally sourced ingredients, are a true culinary delight. Pair your pizza with a craft beer or cider for a complete experience.

Gwesty'r Emlyn Hotel

This elegant hotel houses a restaurant that combines a fine dining experience with the flavors of Wales. Their menu showcases the region's best produce, from succulent meats to fresh seafood. The stylish ambiance and impeccable service create a perfect setting for a special evening out.

Cardigan's Nightlife Scene

While Cardigan's nightlife may not rival major cities, it offers a unique and enjoyable experience. The nightlife here is more about relaxed evenings, live music, and friendly locals.

Theatr Mwldan

This arts and cinema complex is the cultural heart of Cardigan and often hosts live music events. Catch a performance here, and you'll not only enjoy great music but also get a sense of the vibrant local arts scene.

Local Pubs and Bars

Cardigan has a selection of cozy pubs and bars where you can unwind with a pint of local ale or Welsh whisky. These establishments often host quiz nights and live music, providing a laid-back and friendly atmosphere for a night out.

Late-Night Strolls

One of the joys of Cardigan is its peacefulness. Enjoy a late-night stroll along the tranquil riverside or through the quiet streets. The clear night skies are perfect for stargazing, making it a unique way to end your evening.

However, Cardigan Bay's dining and nightlife scene may be more understated compared to larger cities, but it offers a genuine and warm experience that complements the region's natural beauty.

Accommodation in Cardigan

Hotels in Cardigan

Cardigan boasts a selection of charming hotels, each offering a unique experience. The town's hotels cater to a variety of tastes, from cozy boutique establishments to more upscale options. The choice is yours, and it largely depends on your comfort level and budget.

Gwesty'r Webley Hotel - Nestled in the heart of Cardigan, this family-run hotel offers a warm and welcoming atmosphere. With comfortable rooms and a traditional Welsh restaurant, it's an excellent choice for those seeking a taste of local culture. Prices typically range from $90 to $150 per night.

The Cliff Hotel & Spa - For a touch of luxury, consider The Cliff Hotel & Spa, situated overlooking Cardigan Bay. This four-star hotel offers breathtaking sea views, a spa, and a fine dining experience. Expect to pay between $150 and $250 per night for a room here.

Cardigan Castle - For a truly unique experience, consider staying at Cardigan Castle. This historic site offers self-catering accommodation in the heart of the town. You can book one of the castle's self-contained apartments or cottages, with prices starting from $100 per night.

Bed and Breakfasts (B&Bs) in Cardigan

If you prefer a more intimate and personalized experience, Cardigan's B&Bs provide an excellent alternative to hotels. You'll often find warm hospitality and local insights from your hosts.

Highbury B&B - Located near the town center, Highbury B&B offers comfortable rooms and a delicious breakfast. Prices for a room typically range from $80 to $120 per night.

Ty-Parc Guest House - This charming guest house is just a short drive from Cardigan and offers a tranquil setting. Expect to pay between $90 and $150 per night.

Troedyrhiw Holiday Cottages - If you're traveling with a group or prefer self-catering, Troedyrhiw Holiday Cottages provide a range of options, from cozy cottages to larger accommodations. Prices vary based on the size and features of the cottage, starting from $80 per night.

Camping and Caravan Sites

For those who love the great outdoors, Cardigan Bay offers several camping and caravan sites. These options provide a closer connection to nature and are often more budget-friendly.

Poppit Sands Holiday Park - Situated near the stunning Poppit Sands beach, this holiday park offers camping and caravan pitches.

Prices vary depending on the season and amenities, but you can generally expect rates starting at $20 per night.

Cardigan Bay Camping and Caravan Park - This family-friendly park provides spacious pitches and modern facilities. Prices start at around $25 per night.

Penlon Cottage Caravan Park - If you prefer a quieter retreat, Penlon Cottage Caravan Park is set in a peaceful countryside location. Rates for pitches begin at approximately $20 per night.

Therefore, Cardigan provides a range of accommodation options to suit every traveler's needs. Whether you're looking for a luxurious hotel stay, the warmth of a B&B, or the adventure of camping, you'll find a place to call home during your visit. Prices can vary based on the season and specific amenities, so it's advisable to book in advance and check for any special offers or packages available. Your choice of accommodation can significantly enhance your overall experience in this stunning region, ensuring your stay is as memorable as the natural beauty that surrounds you.

In conclusion, exploring the coastal towns of Aberystwyth, New Quay, and Cardigan along the stunning shores of Cardigan Bay offers a diverse array of experiences for travelers.

Aberystwyth presents a unique blend of history and natural beauty. Visitors can immerse themselves in its rich heritage by exploring attractions like the National Library of Wales and Aberystwyth Castle. The town's vibrant dining scene showcases a range of cuisines to suit all tastes, and its nightlife offers a lively atmosphere. Accommodation options are plentiful, from quaint B&Bs to comfortable hotels, ensuring a pleasant stay.

New Quay, with its picturesque harbor and dolphin-spotting opportunities, provides a tranquil coastal escape. The town's attractions include boat trips to observe marine life and the charming Dylan Thomas Trail. Dining options feature fresh seafood, while cozy accommodations enhance the seaside experience.

Cardigan, a historic town steeped in culture, beckons with attractions such as Cardigan Castle and scenic hiking trails. Its dining scene showcases Welsh culinary delights, and diverse accommodation options cater to various preferences.

Each of these coastal towns contributes a unique flavor to the Cardigan Bay experience, ensuring that travelers can savor the beauty, culture, and hospitality of this enchanting region.

Chapter 3

Discovering the Beaches

Cardigan Bay boasts a treasure trove of pristine beaches, each with its unique charm. As you embark on your journey through this enchanting region, I invite you to discover the coastal wonders that await. Let's get into the first gem on our beach-hopping adventure: Mwnt Beach.

Mwnt Beach

Located along the picturesque Ceredigion coastline, Mwnt Beach is a hidden paradise waiting to be explored. With its golden sands and sweeping vistas, this beach is a quintessential example of Cardigan Bay's natural beauty.

Beach Highlights

Mwnt Beach is renowned for its unspoiled and rugged landscape. As you set foot on the shoreline, you'll be greeted by a sense of tranquility that can only be found in such pristine surroundings. The horseshoe-shaped bay, framed by lush green hills, offers a truly postcard-worthy view.

One of the standout features of Mwnt Beach is its historical significance. The tiny white chapel of St. Mary's, perched on the cliffs above the beach, adds a touch of mystique to the landscape.

Legend has it that this chapel was built by angels, and its aura of serenity is undeniable.

Activities and Water Sports

While Mwnt Beach may be a haven of tranquility, it's also a playground for outdoor enthusiasts. If you're a fan of water sports, you're in for a treat. The clear waters of Cardigan Bay are perfect for swimming, kayaking, and paddleboarding. You can rent equipment from local providers, making it easy to dive into the aquatic adventures that await.

For those who prefer to keep their feet on dry land, Mwnt Beach offers excellent hiking opportunities. Follow the coastal path that meanders along the cliffs, providing breathtaking panoramic views of the bay and the chance to spot wildlife such as seals and seabirds.

Facilities

Mwnt Beach may feel like a remote escape, but it's well-equipped to ensure your comfort during your visit. There are public restrooms and ample parking nearby, making it accessible for families and solo travelers alike. However, the lack of commercial development adds to its charm, allowing you to savor the unspoiled beauty of the landscape.

Now that you've uncovered the secrets of Mwnt Beach, your journey through Cardigan Bay continues. In the next section, you'll set your sights on another coastal gem, Poppit Sands, and uncover the treasures it holds.

Poppit Sands: A Coastal Gem

Beach Highlights

As you step onto Poppit Sands, you're greeted by a vast expanse of golden sands that seem to stretch endlessly in both directions. The beach, with its gently sloping terrain, offers an inviting welcome for families and beachcombers alike. The crystal-clear waters of Cardigan Bay lap gently at the shore, creating a serene and inviting atmosphere.

One of the standout features of Poppit Sands is its Blue Flag status, a testament to its cleanliness and water quality. This designation ensures that you can enjoy a safe and refreshing swim in the sea. It's worth noting that the bay here enjoys a milder climate than many other parts of the UK, thanks to the Gulf Stream, making it ideal for a dip even on slightly cooler days.

For nature enthusiasts, Poppit Sands is an excellent spot for birdwatching. The nearby Teifi Estuary is home to a diverse range of bird species, making it a birdwatcher's paradise. You may spot various wading birds, including curlews and oystercatchers, as well as the occasional glimpse of grey seals basking in the sun.

Activities and Water Sports

Poppit Sands is not just a place to relax on the beach. It's also a hub for various water-based activities and sports. Whether you're an adrenaline junkie or prefer a more leisurely approach, there's something for everyone here.

Surfing is a popular pastime at Poppit Sands. The gentle, rolling waves provide an excellent opportunity for both beginners and experienced surfers to catch some waves. If you're new to the sport, you can even find local surf schools that offer lessons and equipment rental.

Kayaking and paddleboarding are also popular activities here. The calm waters of the estuary are perfect for exploring at a leisurely pace. You can rent kayaks or paddleboards locally and embark on your adventure. Don't forget your binoculars; you might encounter some of the area's resident wildlife during your exploration.

Facilities

To ensure your day at Poppit Sands is comfortable and hassle-free, the beach provides a range of essential facilities. Clean public toilets are available, so you won't have to worry about finding a restroom during your visit. Additionally, you'll find ample parking nearby, so you can easily access the beach without a long trek.

If you didn't pack a picnic, there's no need to fret. The beach boasts a charming café where you can savor a variety of snacks, refreshments, and light meals. It's the perfect spot to indulge in a cup of tea and some delicious local treats while enjoying stunning views of the bay.

For those traveling with little ones, Poppit Sands is a family-friendly destination. The beach is patrolled by lifeguards during the peak season, providing peace of mind for parents. Moreover, the gently sloping sands and shallow waters make it safe and enjoyable for children to paddle and play.

Thus, Poppit Sands is a must-visit destination in Cardigan Bay, offering a harmonious blend of natural beauty, recreational opportunities, and essential amenities. Whether you're seeking relaxation on the golden sands, water adventures, or the chance to immerse yourself in the area's rich wildlife, Poppit Sands has something special to offer.

Llangrannog Beach

When you find yourself exploring the picturesque region of Cardigan Bay, your journey will undoubtedly lead you to a wealth of stunning beaches, each with its unique charm. Among these coastal treasures, Llangrannog Beach stands out as a hidden gem, beckoning travelers to its sandy shores. In this guide, we'll take you on a journey to discover the beauty of Llangrannog Beach, from its highlights to the various activities and water sports it offers, as well as the essential facilities that make your visit comfortable and enjoyable.

Llangrannog Beach Highlights

Llangrannog Beach, tucked away on the west coast of Wales, is a true embodiment of natural beauty. This serene beach stretches out along a horseshoe-shaped cove, cradling its visitors in a picturesque embrace. As you arrive, you'll be greeted by the gentle lapping of waves against the shore and the soft, golden sands beneath your feet.

The surrounding cliffs, cloaked in lush greenery, add to the sense of seclusion and tranquility. The clear waters of Cardigan Bay here are inviting, often revealing glimpses of marine life beneath the surface. It's not uncommon to spot playful dolphins or curious seals frolicking in the bay.

Llangrannog Beach is an ideal spot for beachcombers and nature enthusiasts. You can spend hours exploring the unique rock formations and sea caves that dot the coastline. These natural wonders are not only a visual delight but also provide a glimpse into the geological history of the area.

For those who seek a peaceful escape from the hustle and bustle of daily life, Llangrannog Beach offers a quiet sanctuary where you can bask in the sun's warmth, listen to the soothing sounds of the sea, and simply unwind.

Activities and Water Sports

While Llangrannog Beach is perfect for relaxation, it also offers a range of activities and water sports to cater to the adventurous spirit within you. Whether you're a seasoned water sports enthusiast or a novice looking for some aquatic fun, there's something for everyone here.

Surfing: The bay's gentle waves and consistent swells make it an excellent spot for surfing. If you're new to the sport, local surf schools offer lessons, ensuring you catch your first wave safely.

Kayaking and Paddleboarding: Explore the coastline from a different perspective by renting a kayak or paddleboard. Paddle at your own pace, taking in the stunning cliffs and hidden coves along the way.

Snorkeling and Diving: Beneath the clear waters of Llangrannog Beach lies a thriving marine ecosystem. Strap on your snorkel or diving gear and get up close with colorful fish, crabs, and even the occasional seahorse.

Coasteering: For the ultimate adrenaline rush, try coasteering. This adventurous activity involves traversing the coastline, climbing rocks, and leaping into the sea. It's an exhilarating way to experience the rugged beauty of the Cardigan Bay coastline.

Facilities at Llangrannog Beach

To ensure your visit to Llangrannog Beach is both comfortable and enjoyable, the area provides a range of essential facilities.

Parking: Convenient parking areas are available near the beach, making it easy for you to access this coastal haven. It's best to arrive early during peak seasons to secure a parking space.

Cafes and Restaurants: When hunger strikes, you'll find charming cafes and restaurants nearby, offering delicious local cuisine and refreshing beverages. Don't miss the opportunity to savor fresh seafood dishes while enjoying ocean views.

Public Restrooms and Showers: Clean and well-maintained public restrooms and outdoor showers are provided, allowing you to rinse off the sand and saltwater after a day of beach activities.

Lifeguard Services: For peace of mind, lifeguard services operate during the peak season, ensuring the safety of beachgoers.

Thus, Llangrannog Beach is a hidden gem along Cardigan Bay's shores that offers a perfect blend of natural beauty, exciting activities, and essential facilities. Whether you're seeking relaxation or adventure, this serene coastal spot invites you to create cherished memories against a backdrop of stunning cliffs, golden sands, and the soothing rhythm of the sea. So, as you explore Cardigan Bay, make sure to include Llangrannog Beach in your itinerary, and let its beauty and charm captivate your senses.

In conclusion, Cardigan Bay boasts a trio of stunning beaches, each with its unique allure.

Mwnt Beach captivates with its unspoiled beauty, offering a serene escape from the world. Its remarkable highlights include panoramic views of rolling hills and a charming historic church overlooking the bay. While here, you can revel in nature's wonders, spot dolphins playing offshore, and explore intriguing rock formations.

At Poppit Sands, the expansive golden shoreline stretches as far as the eye can see, making it a paradise for beach lovers. The highlights encompass its sheer size and a backdrop of lush dunes. The beach also beckons water sports enthusiasts with excellent conditions for surfing, kayaking, and paddleboarding. Facilities like ample parking and cafes ensure a convenient visit.

Finally, Llangrannog Beach enchants visitors with its secluded cove and pristine waters. It offers a tranquil retreat amidst towering cliffs and boasts remarkable natural highlights. Adventure-seekers can partake in surfing, snorkeling, and coasteering. Essential facilities such as parking, dining options, and lifeguard services provide a comfortable beach experience.

In this trio of coastal gems, Cardigan Bay truly offers something for every beachgoer, from serenity to adventure, ensuring unforgettable memories along its breathtaking shores.

Chapter 4

Exploring the National Parks

Located in the heart of the stunning Cardigan Bay region, you'll discover an abundance of natural beauty waiting to be explored. As we delve into the National Parks that grace this area, we'll begin with the majestic Snowdonia National Park. This pristine wilderness offers an array of experiences, from serene hikes to encounters with remarkable wildlife.

Snowdonia National Park

Snowdonia National Park, occupying a vast expanse of 823 square miles, is a true gem within Cardigan Bay. Its breathtaking landscapes encompass rugged mountains, tranquil lakes, and enchanting forests, making it a haven for nature enthusiasts and adventure seekers alike. Let's go on a journey through this magnificent park.

Hiking Trails

When it comes to hiking, Snowdonia National Park is a paradise for outdoor enthusiasts. The park is home to the highest mountain in Wales, Mount Snowdon, standing proudly at 3,560 feet. A hike to its summit rewards you with panoramic views that stretch as far as the eye can see. The journey to the top is an adventure in itself, with several routes of varying difficulty levels. The Pyg Track offers a challenging ascent, while the Llanberis Path provides a more leisurely option.

But Snowdon isn't the only highlight. Explore the Carneddau Range, where rugged peaks and tranquil valleys create a playground for seasoned hikers. The Glyderau, with its distinctive rocky formations, offers a unique experience. And don't forget about the picturesque Moel Siabod, a mountain that boasts exceptional views of the surrounding countryside.

As you hike through Snowdonia, keep an eye out for the diverse flora and fauna that call this park home. From vibrant wildflowers carpeting the meadows to the elusive peregrine falcon soaring above, the natural world here is a delight for all ages.

Wildlife and Nature

The biodiversity of Snowdonia National Park is nothing short of remarkable. Its pristine habitats support a wide range of wildlife, from the tiniest insects to majestic birds of prey. As you explore the park, you may encounter red squirrels darting through the woodlands or glimpse a graceful otter along the banks of a crystal-clear river.

Birdwatchers will be in their element, with Snowdonia hosting a variety of species. The peregrine falcon, with its impressive hunting skills, can often be spotted in the skies. Keep an ear out for the haunting calls of the raven echoing across the rugged terrain. And in the wetlands, you might catch a glimpse of a kingfisher's vibrant flash of blue as it dives for its prey.

For those with a keen interest in botany, Snowdonia doesn't disappoint. Rare and delicate wildflowers adorn the landscape, creating a vibrant tapestry of color during the warmer months. The park's ancient oak and pine forests are a testament to its rich natural history.

In the heart of Snowdonia, you'll find hidden gems like Cwm Idwal, a glacial cirque boasting an extraordinary variety of alpine plants. The tranquil Glaslyn Nature Reserve is a birdwatcher's paradise, ding a safe haven for ospreys and other avian wonders.

Whether you're an avid hiker, a wildlife enthusiast, or simply seeking solace in nature's beauty, Snowdonia National Park offers an unforgettable experience. The enchanting landscapes and rich biodiversity will leave you with memories to cherish forever.

Pembrokeshire Coast National Park

Pembrokeshire Coast National Park is a gem nestled along the rugged western coastline of Wales, and it's a place where nature truly shows off its finest artistry. This pristine park extends over 600 square kilometers, making it one of the most extensive and diverse protected areas in the United Kingdom. Whether you're a nature enthusiast, a hiker, or simply seeking a tranquil escape, Pembrokeshire Coast National Park beckons you with its allure.

At the heart of this magnificent park lies a mosaic of landscapes, with its own unique charm. From towering cliffs that plunge dramatically into the Atlantic Ocean to secluded coves and sandy beaches, Pembrokeshire's scenery is nothing short of awe-inspiring. The park's diverse ecosystems, ranging from ancient woodlands to windswept moorlands, create a haven for an array of wildlife. As you embark on your journey through this natural wonder, be prepared to be captivated by its beauty at every turn.

Coastal Walks

One of the best ways to immerse yourself in the splendor of Pembrokeshire Coast National Park is by embarking on its legendary coastal walks. The park boasts a network of paths and trails that span over 300 kilometers, offering something for hikers of all levels. Whether you're an avid trekker or stroller, these routes cater to everyone.

The Pembrokeshire Coast Path, a 186-mile trail that hugs the cliff edges, is an icon among long-distance walkers. It presents a challenge, but the rewards are boundless. As you traverse this path, you'll be treated to uninterrupted vistas of the wild coastline, with seabirds wheeling overhead and the scent of salt in the air. It's an adventure that will etch memories into your soul.

For those seeking shorter excursions, consider exploring stretches of the path or taking circular walks within the park. The beauty of Pembrokeshire Coast National Park is that you can tailor your experience to your preferences. You might find yourself meandering through ancient woodlands one day and following the coastline the next, always immersed in nature's grandeur.

Birdwatching

Birdwatching in Pembrokeshire Coast National Park is a delight for both seasoned birdwatchers and novices. This region is a thriving hub of avian activity, owing to its diverse habitats that range from cliff faces to estuaries. The park's geographical location, jutting out into the Irish Sea, also makes it a significant stopover point for migratory birds.

One of the avian stars of the park is the Atlantic puffin. Skomer Island, just off the coast, is a renowned breeding ground for these charismatic seabirds. Visiting Skomer during the breeding season offers a chance to witness thousands of puffins bustling about, caring for their young. It's a spectacle that will leave you enchanted.

Beyond puffins, Pembrokeshire Coast National Park hosts a wealth of other bird species. Keep an eye out for choughs, peregrine falcons, and kestrels soaring along the cliffs. The wetlands and estuaries provide a habitat for waders like oystercatchers and curlews, adding to the diversity of sightings. Don't forget your binoculars and camera, for every corner of this park has the potential to reveal avian wonders.

Thus, Pembrokeshire Coast National Park is a treasure trove of natural wonders. Its dramatic landscapes, coastal walks, and birdwatching opportunities make it a must-visit destination within the Cardigan Bay region. Whether you're drawn by the thrill of hiking along the cliff edges or the serenity of birdwatching, this park has something truly special to offer.

Exploring the remarkable National Parks of Cardigan Bay, Snowdonia National Park, and Pembrokeshire Coast National Park stand out as jewels in this coastal crown.

Snowdonia National Park presents a captivating overview of rugged terrain, with the majestic Mount Snowdon at its heart. It's a landscape that invites adventure, from challenging hikes to tranquil lakeside strolls. The hiking trails here lead you through a tapestry of natural beauty, with every step revealing the splendors of ancient woodlands, cascading waterfalls, and awe-inspiring peaks. Amidst this stunning backdrop, wildlife thrives, offering glimpses of elusive creatures like red squirrels and peregrine falcons. Snowdonia is a testament to nature's resilience and grandeur.

Pembrokeshire Coast National Park enchants with its dramatic coastal beauty. The overview is a mosaic of landscapes, from towering cliffs to secluded coves. Coastal walks here are legendary, offering vistas that linger in memory. Birdwatching enthusiasts find a haven, with puffins and other seabirds gracing its shores. It's a place where nature's artistry is showcased in every view.

Both these national parks beckon adventurers, nature enthusiasts, and wanderers alike. They are an embodiment of Cardigan Bay's allure, promising unforgettable experiences for those who heed their call.

Chapter 5

Experiencing Wildlife

Cardigan Bay is a region renowned for its stunning landscapes and rich biodiversity, making it a haven for wildlife enthusiasts. Here, I'll delve into the incredible world of Cardigan Bay's wildlife, focusing on dolphin and seal watching, the best spots to witness these majestic creatures in their natural habitat, Guided Tours, and Conservation Efforts

Dolphin and Seal Watching

One of the most thrilling experiences you can have in Cardigan Bay is observing its vibrant marine life. The bay is home to a variety of marine mammals, with dolphins and seals taking center stage in this mesmerizing aquatic spectacle. As you embark on your wildlife adventure, prepare to be captivated by the playful antics of dolphins and the serene grace of seals.

Best Spots

Cardigan Bay's extensive coastline offers numerous vantage points for observing dolphins and seals, but some areas stand out as the best spots for these encounters. Here, we'll explore a few of these prime locations, where your chances of witnessing these incredible animals are particularly high.

Aberystwyth

Aberystwyth, a charming coastal town nestled on the shores of Cardigan Bay, is a fantastic starting point for your wildlife expedition. The town's picturesque promenade provides an excellent vantage point for spotting dolphins, especially during the summer months. The bottlenose dolphins, often seen in these waters, are known for their acrobatic displays, leaping out of the water with seemingly boundless energy.

New Quay

New Quay, another coastal gem, is renowned as a hub for marine life enthusiasts. The town boasts a resident population of bottlenose dolphins, making it an ideal location for dolphin watching. Several boat tours operate from New Quay, taking you out to sea where you can witness these intelligent creatures in their natural habitat. Keep your camera ready; you won't want to miss capturing these remarkable moments.

Cardigan Island Coastal Farm Park

For a more secluded and nature-immersive experience, consider a visit to Cardigan Island Coastal Farm Park. Situated on a headland overlooking Cardigan Bay, this park provides a unique opportunity to observe seals in their natural environment. Grey seals are commonly spotted here, and you can witness their endearing antics, from sunbathing on rocky outcrops to playfully bobbing in the waves.

Pembrokeshire Coast National Park

While not directly in Cardigan Bay, the Pembrokeshire Coast National Park is a short drive away and offers exceptional wildlife encounters. Boat tours departing from towns like Tenby often venture into these waters, increasing your chances of spotting dolphins and seals. The park's rugged cliffs and pristine beaches also provide excellent vantage points for observing these magnificent creatures.

Cardigan Bay Marine Wildlife Centre

The Cardigan Bay Marine Wildlife Centre, based in New Quay, serves as an invaluable resource for wildlife enthusiasts. Here, you can learn more about the marine life that inhabits Cardigan Bay, and the knowledgeable staff can provide insights into the best times and locations for sightings. They also offer guided walks and talks, enhancing your understanding of the bay's unique ecosystem.

When you set out to witness Cardigan Bay's dolphins and seals, remember to respect their natural habitat by maintaining a safe distance and avoiding any disturbance. Bring binoculars and a camera with a good zoom lens to capture these moments without intruding on their space.

Guided Tours

To enhance your dolphin and seal-watching experience in Cardigan Bay, consider joining one of the many guided tours available in the area. These tours offer not only a deeper understanding of marine life but also the opportunity to interact with knowledgeable guides who can share fascinating insights.

Dolphin and Seal-Watching Tours

Several tour operators in towns like New Quay and Aberystwyth offer specialized dolphin and seal-watching excursions. These tours are designed to maximize your chances of encountering these marine mammals. Knowledgeable guides, often with years of experience, accompany you on these outings, ensuring you're in the right place at the right time.

During these tours, guides provide valuable information about the behavior and habits of dolphins and seals. They can identify individual dolphins based on unique markings and share stories about the local marine residents. This level of expertise elevates the experience, making it educational as well as awe-inspiring.

Interactive Experiences

For an even more immersive encounter with Cardigan Bay's wildlife, some tours offer interactive experiences. Depending on the operator, you may have the opportunity to snorkel alongside seals or participate in research efforts to monitor and protect these creatures. These experiences not only provide unforgettable memories but also contribute to conservation efforts.

Conservation Efforts

The health and preservation of Cardigan Bay's marine life are paramount to the region's identity and ecosystem. Efforts to protect and conserve dolphins, seals, and other marine species are ongoing, and your visit can play a part in supporting these initiatives.

Research and Monitoring

Various organizations, such as the Cardigan Bay Marine Wildlife Centre, actively engage in research and monitoring programs. These initiatives collect valuable data on the behavior and population dynamics of dolphins and seals. By participating in guided tours or interactive experiences, you contribute to these efforts, as a portion of the proceeds often go toward funding research and conservation projects.

Educational Outreach

Conservation efforts extend to educational outreach programs aimed at raising awareness about the importance of preserving Cardigan Bay's marine life. The Cardigan Bay Marine Wildlife Centre, for example, conducts workshops, talks, and school visits to educate both locals and visitors about the bay's fragile ecosystem. Your visit can help support these educational initiatives, ensuring that future generations appreciate and protect this unique environment.

Responsible Wildlife Watching

While experiencing the wonder of dolphins and seals in Cardigan Bay, it's crucial to do so responsibly. Tour operators adhere to strict guidelines to minimize disturbance to these animals. Following their instructions, such as maintaining a safe distance and avoiding loud noises, ensures that your presence has no negative impact on marine life.

Thus, dolphin and seal watching in Cardigan Bay offers not only a chance to witness the beauty of these creatures but also an opportunity to contribute to their conservation. Guided tours enhance your experience, and your participation supports ongoing research and educational efforts. By embracing responsible wildlife-watching practices, you play a role in safeguarding the marine life that makes Cardigan Bay a truly extraordinary destination.

Birdwatching

Cardigan Bay, with its diverse ecosystems and stunning natural beauty, is a birdwatcher's paradise. The region's unique combination of coastal habitats, wetlands, and woodlands makes it a haven for a wide variety of avian species. Let's explore the world of birdwatching in Cardigan Bay, focusing on the notable bird species you can encounter here.

Notable Bird Species

Cardigan Bay's rich biodiversity extends to its birdlife, and whether you're a seasoned birder or just starting out, you're in for a treat. Here, we'll introduce you to some of the most remarkable bird species you can spot in the region.

Chough (*Pyrrhocorax pyrrhocorax*): The chough is a distinctive and charismatic bird known for its vibrant red bill and legs. This species thrives along the rugged cliffs of Cardigan Bay, where it performs impressive aerial displays. Keep an eye out for their acrobatic flights and melodious calls as they cruise above the coastline.

Peregrine Falcon (Falco peregrinus): The Peregrine Falcon, renowned for its incredible speed and hunting prowess, is a common sight in Cardigan Bay. These raptors often nest on cliffs, and you might witness their breathtaking stoop as they dive at high speeds to catch prey.

Red Kite (*Milvus milvus*): With its distinctive forked tail and striking reddish-brown plumage, the Red Kite is a symbol of conservation success in Wales. Cardigan Bay provides an ideal habitat for these graceful birds of prey, and you can often spot them soaring overhead.

Osprey (*Pandion haliaetus*): The Cardigan Bay region is home to a growing population of Ospreys. These large, fish-eating raptors are known for their stunning aerial displays while hunting. They can be seen hovering over the bay before making dramatic dives into the water to catch their prey.

Little Tern (Sternula albifrons): For those interested in coastal birdwatching, the Little Tern is a delightful find. These small, white terns with distinctive black caps nest on sandy beaches along Cardigan Bay. Witness their delicate and agile fishing flights close to the shoreline.

Curlew (Numenius arquata): The haunting call of the Curlew is a familiar sound in Cardigan Bay's estuaries and wetlands. These large waders with their long, curved bills are often seen foraging in the mudflats during low tide.

Kingfisher (Alcedo atthis): Cardigan Bay's waterways and rivers are the domain of the vibrant Kingfisher. With their brilliant blue and orange plumage, these small birds are a delight to observe as they dart above the water, hunting for fish.

Mute Swan (Cygnus olor): The graceful Mute Swans are a common sight on Cardigan Bay's tranquil lakes and rivers. Their pure white plumage and distinctive curved necks make for a serene and picturesque scene.

When you embark on your birdwatching adventure in Cardigan Bay, remember to bring your binoculars and a field guide to identify these and many other avian residents. The best times for birdwatching are during the early morning or late afternoon when many birds are active.

Birding Hotspots

In your quest for birdwatching excellence in Cardigan Bay, it's essential to know where to find the best birding hotspots. The region offers a variety of habitats, each with its unique feathered inhabitants. Here, I'll guide you through some of the prime locations to observe these avian wonders.

Pembrokeshire Coast National Park: This national park is not only known for its breathtaking coastal scenery but also for its diverse birdlife. Head to spots like Skomer Island and the Marloes Peninsula to catch glimpses of puffins, guillemots, and razorbills nesting on the cliffs. The heathlands and wetlands within the park are also home to numerous species, including the iconic chough.

Cors Fochno (Borth Bog): If wetland birds fascinate you, Cors Fochno, a large peat bog near Borth, is a must-visit. Here, you can spot a variety of waders, waterfowl, and elusive species like the Eurasian Bittern. The boardwalks and hides make it easier to observe the avian residents without disturbing them.

Aberystwyth: This coastal town is not only a charming destination but also a great birding hotspot. Stroll along the Promenade, and you may encounter turnstones, oystercatchers, and even seals. The

Rheidol River estuary is another fantastic place for birdwatching, with its resident curlews and redshanks.

Dyfi Osprey Project: For a close encounter with Ospreys, head to the Dyfi Osprey Project near Machynlleth. This conservation initiative offers fantastic opportunities to watch these magnificent birds in their nests via live-streaming cameras.

Cardigan Island Coastal Farm Park: Located near Gwbert, this coastal farm park is a haven for seabird enthusiasts. Take a boat trip to Cardigan Island, where you can observe a plethora of species, including guillemots, razorbills, and Atlantic grey seals.

Teifi Marshes Nature Reserve: Situated near Cardigan, this reserve offers a tranquil setting for birdwatching. Explore the reedbeds, ponds, and wet grasslands to spot birds like the water rail, reed warbler, and teal. The observation hides provide excellent vantage points for bird enthusiasts.

Birdwatching Tours

While exploring Cardigan Bay independently can be a rewarding experience, joining a birdwatching tour can enhance your adventure. These guided tours are led by experts who know the region's avian residents and their habits intimately. Here's what you can expect from birdwatching tours in Cardigan Bay:

Expert Guidance: Knowledgeable guides will accompany you, sharing insights about the bird species you encounter, their behavior, and the best times to observe them.

Access to Exclusive Locations: Birdwatching tours often have access to private or restricted areas where you can observe rare and elusive species.

Quality Equipment: Many tours provide binoculars and spotting scopes, ensuring you get a close-up view of the birds without the need for your equipment.

Safety and Conservation: Tours prioritize the well-being of the birds and their habitats, ensuring minimal disturbance while you enjoy your birdwatching experience.

Photography Opportunities: If you're an avid bird photographer, some tours cater to your interests, offering tips and opportunities for capturing stunning avian moments.

Educational Experience: Beyond birdwatching, tours often provide valuable information about the broader ecosystem and conservation efforts in Cardigan Bay.

When choosing a birdwatching tour, consider your interests, whether you prefer coastal, wetland, or woodland birding. With these tours, you'll have the opportunity to witness the beauty and diversity of Cardigan Bay's avian inhabitants while benefiting from the expertise of experienced guides.

In conclusion, experiencing wildlife in Cardigan Bay is an enchanting journey into the heart of nature's wonders. Dolphin and seal watching are among the most thrilling encounters, with the bay's clear waters providing a perfect stage for these marine marvels. The best spots, including New Quay and Cardigan Island, offer front-row seats to these mesmerizing spectacles.

Guided tours elevate your wildlife experience, with knowledgeable experts sharing their passion and insights. These tours not only enhance your understanding of the region's biodiversity but also ensure responsible and ethical wildlife encounters.

Conservation efforts play a crucial role in preserving the rich marine life of Cardigan Bay. Initiatives like the Dyfi Osprey Project and coastal clean-up campaigns demonstrate a commitment to safeguarding these habitats for future generations.

Birdwatching enthusiasts will be captivated by the notable bird species and birding hotspots. From the graceful Osprey to the elusive Bittern, Cardigan Bay's diverse avian residents provide endless opportunities for observation.

Birdwatching tours, led by experts, offer a deeper connection to the feathered inhabitants of the region, making every sighting a memorable experience. In Cardigan Bay, the harmonious coexistence of wildlife and humans is a testament to the beauty and importance of conservation efforts, ensuring that this stunning region remains a sanctuary for both wildlife and those who seek to admire it.

Chapter 6

Outdoor Adventures

Cardigan Bay is a haven for outdoor enthusiasts, offering a wide range of adventures that cater to every interest. Whether you're an avid hiker, a nature lover, or simply seeking an escape from the hustle and bustle of city life, you'll find something here that speaks to your soul.

Hiking and Walking

Hiking and walking in Cardigan Bay are experiences that will leave you breathless, both from the physical exertion and the breathtaking scenery. This region boasts a myriad of trails that wind through coastal cliffs, ancient woodlands, and picturesque countryside. Lace up your walking boots, and let's explore some of the top trails that Cardigan Bay has to offer.

Top Trails

Ceredigion Coast Path: Stretching for over 60 miles, the Ceredigion Coast Path offers a fantastic opportunity to explore the entire length of Cardigan Bay's coastline. This trail provides a spectacular vantage point for observing the bay's diverse marine life. Keep an eye out for dolphins and seals playing in the waves below as you traverse this rugged path.

Pembrokeshire Coast Path: Although slightly south of Cardigan Bay, the Pembrokeshire Coast Path is an iconic Welsh trail that's well worth the visit. The section near Cardigan Bay offers stunning views of the rugged coastline and access to hidden coves and sandy beaches.

Llandysul and Pont-Tyweli Walk: For a more relaxed stroll, consider the Llandysul and Pont-Tyweli Walk. This riverside path is perfect for families and offers a glimpse into the tranquil countryside surrounding the bay.

Difficulty Levels

Cardigan Bay's trails cater to hikers of all skill levels, from beginners to seasoned adventurers. Here, you'll find trails that are as easy-going as a leisurely walk along the beach and others that will test your endurance and determination.

Easy Trails: If you're new to hiking or simply want a leisurely walk, explore the gentle pathways around the coastal towns. The Aberystwyth Promenade offers a picturesque seaside stroll, complete with charming cafes where you can pause for a cup of tea.

Moderate Trails: For those seeking a bit more challenge, the trails in the nearby national parks, such as Pembrokeshire Coast and Snowdonia, offer moderate difficulty levels. The terrain varies from undulating coastal paths to lush forests, providing a diverse range of experiences.

Challenging Trails: If you're an experienced hiker, tackle the more strenuous trails, like the Ceredigion Coast Path or the challenging sections of the Pembrokeshire Coast Path. These paths include steep ascents, uneven terrain, and longer distances, but the rewards in terms of scenery are unparalleled.

Cardigan Bay caters to every kind of hiker, making it an ideal destination for anyone looking to explore the great outdoors at their own pace.

As you explore Cardigan Bay's hiking trails, remember to respect the natural environment and adhere to the Leave No Trace principles. This ensures that future generations can continue to enjoy the pristine beauty of this remarkable coastline.

Safety Tips

Safety should always be a top priority when you're embarking on hiking and walking adventures in Cardigan Bay. While this stunning region offers unparalleled natural beauty, it also presents unique challenges that you need to be aware of. Here are some essential safety tips to ensure your outdoor explorations are both enjoyable and secure:

Plan Your Route: Before setting out on any hike or walk, plan your route thoroughly. Familiarize yourself with the trail, its length, and any potential hazards. Cardigan Bay's coastal paths can be quite remote in some areas, so ensure you have a map or GPS device with you.

Check the Weather: The weather in Wales can be unpredictable, so check the forecast before heading out. Be prepared for sudden changes in conditions, and dress accordingly with layers that can be added or removed as needed. Always carry a waterproof jacket, even on sunny days.

Stay on Marked Paths: Stick to designated trails and paths, especially in protected areas like national parks. Venturing off-trail can damage fragile ecosystems and pose risks to your safety.

Footwear and Equipment: Invest in a good pair of hiking boots with ankle support and proper grip. Carry essential equipment, including a fully charged mobile phone, a first-aid kit, a whistle, and a headlamp or flashlight with spare batteries.

Hydration and Nutrition: Carry an adequate supply of water and high-energy snacks to keep you hydrated and fueled during your hike. Cardigan Bay's coastal paths may not have frequent access to amenities, so it's essential to be self-sufficient.

Wildlife Awareness: While exploring the trails, you might encounter local wildlife, such as sheep and cattle. Keep a safe distance from these animals, especially if they have young offspring. Be aware of potential encounters with larger wildlife like ponies or seals, and always observe from a distance.

Tides and Coastal Hazards: If your hike takes you close to the shoreline, be mindful of the tides. Some areas may become impassable during high tide, so check tide times and plan accordingly. Watch out for slippery rocks and be cautious around cliff edges.

Emergency Contacts: Save local emergency contact numbers, such as the coastguard or mountain rescue, in your phone before you start your hike. In case of an emergency, call for help as soon as possible.

Leave No Trace: Respect the natural environment by not littering and taking all your trash with you. Follow the Leave No Trace principles to minimize your impact on the landscape.

By following these safety tips, you can fully enjoy the incredible hiking and walking experiences that Cardigan Bay has to offer. It's a place of unspoiled beauty, and with the right precautions, you can explore it safely and responsibly.

Water Sports

Cardigan Bay offers a wealth of opportunities for water sports enthusiasts. Whether you're a seasoned pro or a novice looking to dip your toes into the waters, there's something here for everyone. Now let's delve into the exhilarating world of water sports, beginning with the ever-popular activity of surfing.

Surfing

Surfing in Cardigan Bay is more than just a sport; it's a way of life. The combination of powerful Atlantic swells, consistent waves, and stunning coastal scenery makes this region a mecca for surfers from around the world. As you stand on the golden sands, with the bracing sea breeze in your hair and the sound of crashing waves in the background, you'll understand why Cardigan Bay holds a special place in the hearts of surfers.

Surf Spots

Before you wax up your board and hit the waves, it's essential to know the best surf spots Cardigan Bay has to offer. Here are some notable locations:

- Mwnt Beach: This idyllic cove offers consistent waves, making it ideal for both beginners and experienced surfers. The backdrop of rolling hills and the historic Church of the Holy Cross adds to the charm.

- Poppit Sands: Known for its long sandy beach, Poppit Sands is a great spot for learners. Gentle waves and a welcoming local surf scene make it a perfect place to catch your first wave.
- Traeth Penbryn: With its remote location and pristine waters, Traeth Penbryn provides an excellent setting for those seeking a more secluded surf experience. The waves here can be challenging, attracting more seasoned surfers.
- Other Notable Beaches: Cardigan Bay is dotted with hidden gems, each offering unique surfing experiences. Explore the coastline, and you'll stumble upon secret breaks that could become your personal paradise.

Surf Schools and Rentals

For those new to surfing, or if you want to hone your skills, Cardigan Bay boasts a range of surf schools and equipment rental options. These schools are staffed by experienced instructors who know the local waters like the back of their hand. They'll ensure you have a safe and exhilarating time catching waves.

Surfing Events

Cardigan Bay hosts various surfing events throughout the year, attracting surfers and spectators alike. These competitions showcase the talent of local surfers and often feature live music, food stalls, and a vibrant atmosphere. Be sure to check the local event calendar to see if there's a surf competition happening during your visit.

Surfing Etiquette

As you paddle out into the waves, it's crucial to respect the ocean and your fellow surfers. Cardigan Bay is renowned for its friendly surf community, and adhering to proper surfing etiquette is a must. Always follow the lineup rules, respect the locals, and leave no trace of your visit.

Here, surfing in Cardigan Bay is an experience like no other. Whether you're riding the waves for the first time or chasing that perfect break, the combination of thrilling surf, stunning scenery, and a warm surf culture will leave you with lasting memories. So, grab your board, catch some waves, and immerse yourself in the world of Cardigan Bay surfing. It's a ride you won't forget in a hurry.

Kayaking

As we continue our exploration of water sports in Cardigan Bay, let's paddle our way into the serene world of kayaking. Kayaking offers a unique perspective on this stunning region, allowing you to get up close and personal with its diverse marine life and breathtaking coastal landscapes.

The Tranquil Waters of Cardigan Bay

Cardigan Bay's calm and sheltered waters make it an ideal destination for kayaking enthusiasts of all levels. Whether you're an experienced sea kayaker or a first-time paddler, you'll find plenty of opportunities to explore this pristine marine environment at your own pace.

Exploring Sea Caves and Hidden Coves

One of the most thrilling aspects of kayaking in Cardigan Bay is the chance to discover hidden sea caves and secluded coves along the coastline. Paddle through natural archways and into caves that have been carved by the relentless force of the sea over countless millennia. These hidden gems offer a sense of adventure and wonder that few other activities can match.

Encounters with Marine Life

Cardigan Bay is renowned for its rich marine biodiversity. While kayaking, you may be lucky enough to encounter playful dolphins, curious seals, and a variety of seabirds. The bay is also a protected area for the bottlenose dolphin population, making it one of the best places in the UK to spot these intelligent creatures in their natural habitat.

Kayaking Routes

Numerous kayaking routes crisscross Cardigan Bay, catering to both beginners and experienced paddlers. Here are a few noteworthy options:

Aberystwyth to Borth: This route takes you along the rugged coastline, offering stunning views of Aberystwyth's historic pier and the Cambrian Mountains in the distance.

New Quay to Cwmtydu: Paddle past the charming town of New Quay and venture south to Cwmtydu, a secluded cove known for its resident seal colony.

Aberaeron to Llanon: Explore the picturesque harbor town of Aberaeron and paddle north to Llanon, passing by beautiful beaches and rocky cliffs.

Kayak Rentals and Tours

If you're new to kayaking or simply don't have your equipment, fear not. Cardigan Bay boasts several outfitters that offer kayak rentals and guided tours. These experienced guides can lead you to the best spots, share local knowledge, and ensure your safety while out on the water.

Safety Considerations

While kayaking in Cardigan Bay is generally safe, it's essential to be aware of the ever-changing weather conditions and tidal currents. Always wear a personal flotation device (PFD) and be mindful of your skill level when choosing your kayaking route.

Thus, kayaking in Cardigan Bay offers a peaceful and immersive way to experience the natural beauty and marine life of this remarkable region. Whether you're gliding through hidden caves, observing dolphins at play, or simply enjoying the tranquility of the bay, kayaking here is an unforgettable adventure that will leave you with a deep appreciation for the coastal wonders of Cardigan Bay. So, grab a paddle and embark on your kayaking journey in this stunning part of Wales.

Sailing

In our exploration of water sports in Cardigan Bay, let's now set sail into the realm of sailing. Sailing in Cardigan Bay offers a unique and peaceful way to experience the beauty of the region's coastline and the open sea.

The Sailors' Paradise

Cardigan Bay's vast expanse of open water, reliable winds, and picturesque harbors make it a sailor's paradise. Whether you're a seasoned sailor or a novice looking to learn the ropes, you'll find that Cardigan Bay offers a range of sailing experiences for all levels.

Sailing Schools and Courses

For those new to sailing, there are excellent sailing schools and courses available in the coastal towns around Cardigan Bay. These schools offer expert instruction, teaching you the fundamentals of sailing, navigation, and seamanship. You can choose from short introductory courses or more extensive programs, depending on your level of interest and commitment.

Charming Harbors and Anchorages

Cardigan Bay is dotted with charming harbors and anchorages that beckon sailors to drop anchor and explore the picturesque coastal towns. Aberystwyth, New Quay, and Aberaeron are just a few of the delightful harbors you can visit. These towns offer a warm welcome to sailors and boast excellent facilities, including marinas, restaurants, and pubs.

Sailing Events and Regattas

Throughout the year, Cardigan Bay hosts various sailing events and regattas that attract sailors from near and far. These events provide a fantastic opportunity to join in the excitement, watch competitive racing, or even participate if you're feeling adventurous. The camaraderie among sailors and the lively atmosphere of these events are not to be missed.

Exploring the Coastline

Sailing allows you to explore Cardigan Bay's coastline from a unique perspective. As you glide over the glistening waters, you'll be treated to stunning views of rugged cliffs, pristine beaches, and lush green hillsides. The bay's sheltered waters make it ideal for both relaxed coastal cruising and more challenging offshore adventures.

Wildlife Encounters

Sailing in Cardigan Bay often includes delightful encounters with the local wildlife. Keep an eye out for dolphins and porpoises that frequently swim alongside boats. Seabirds, such as gannets and puffins, can also be spotted during your sail. These wildlife sightings add an extra layer of magic to your sailing experience.

Safety Precautions

Before setting sail in Cardigan Bay, it's crucial to check weather forecasts and tides. Coastal conditions can change rapidly, so it's essential to be prepared and have the necessary safety equipment on board. Always ensure you have life jackets for all passengers, a VHF radio for communication, and a well-maintained vessel.

In conclusion, sailing in Cardigan Bay is a serene and captivating way to connect with the beauty of this coastal region. Whether you're enjoying a cruise along the shoreline or embarking on an adventurous offshore journey, the bay's calm waters and welcoming communities make it an ideal destination for sailors of all backgrounds. So, hoist your sails, feel the wind in your hair, and set off on a sailing adventure that will leave you with lasting memories of Cardigan Bay's maritime magic.

Chapter 7

Cultural and Historical Attractions

Cardigan Bay is a treasure trove of natural beauty and cultural heritage. As you embark on your journey through this stunning region, you'll find an array of cultural and historical attractions that add depth to the experience.

Castles and Historic Sites

Wales is known for its castles, and Cardigan Bay certainly doesn't disappoint in this regard. These imposing structures stand as a testament to the region's storied history, bearing witness to centuries of battles, intrigue, and resilience. One such jewel in Cardigan Bay's historical crown is Cardigan Castle.

Cardigan Castle

Cardigan Castle, perched majestically on the banks of the Teifi River, is a beacon of history and culture in the heart of Cardigan town. Its origins date back to the 12th century when it was founded by the Norman lord Roger de Montgomery. Over the centuries, it has undergone numerous transformations and played pivotal roles in Welsh history.

You step into the castle grounds, and the stone walls whisper tales of knights and nobles. The castle's turbulent past includes sieges, restorations, and even a ghostly legend or two. As you explore the meticulously preserved chambers and courtyards, it's as if you're walking through a living history book.

Cardigan Castle's recent restoration efforts have breathed new life into this ancient edifice. You can't help but admire the dedication to preserving its heritage and making it accessible to visitors like you. The castle is now a cultural hub, hosting events, exhibitions, and performances throughout the year.

Take your time to wander through the Georgian mansion, explore the beautifully landscaped gardens, and learn about the castle's role in the 1176 Battle of Crug Mawr. Don't forget to climb the tower for panoramic views of Cardigan and the Teifi Estuary; the vista is nothing short of breathtaking.

As you stand within the walls of Cardigan Castle, you'll appreciate the fusion of history and contemporary culture that makes this place so special. The castle isn't just a relic of the past; it's a living testament to the enduring spirit of Cardigan Bay and its people.

Beyond Cardigan Castle, Cardigan Bay boasts an array of other historic sites and landmarks waiting to be discovered. Each one has a unique story to tell, whether it's the remnants of ancient hillforts or the stone circles scattered across the landscape.

In this vibrant region where past and present coexist harmoniously, you'll find that every historic site has its charm and significance. As you explore Cardigan Bay's cultural and historical attractions, you'll gain a deeper understanding of the region's identity and the people who have shaped it over the centuries.

Cilgerran Castle

Located on the banks of the Teifi River, Cilgerran Castle stands as a testament to both Welsh and Norman history. This mighty fortress, with its imposing stone walls and commanding presence, offers a captivating journey back in time.

You'll find Cilgerran Castle just a short drive from Cardigan town. As you approach, its silhouette against the sky is enough to capture your imagination. The castle's strategic location, perched atop a steep hill overlooking the river, once made it a formidable stronghold.

Cilgerran Castle's history dates back to the 12th century when it was built by the Norman conquerors. It played a pivotal role in the struggles for control of this region, witnessing battles and sieges that have become legendary. The site, however, also has ancient Welsh roots, adding an intriguing layer of cultural significance.

Exploring the castle grounds today, you can wander through its well-preserved ruins, climb the stone steps to the top of the towers, and take in panoramic views of the Teifi River valley. The visitor center provides informative displays and insights into the castle's history, making your visit both educational and engaging.

Cilgerran Castle has not only a strategic but also a picturesque location, surrounded by lush greenery and the serene flow of the river below. It's a fantastic spot for photographers and history enthusiasts alike.

When you visit, take your time to absorb the atmosphere and imagine the lives of those who once inhabited these stone walls. Picture the knights and nobles who roamed these halls, the battles fought, and the stories woven into every stone.

As you leave Cilgerran Castle behind, you'll carry with you not just memories of a historic site but a deeper appreciation for the layers of history that Cardigan Bay holds within its embrace.

Cardigan Bay is a region that continues to beckon travelers with its rich history, stunning landscapes, and vibrant culture. As you explore its castles and historic sites, you'll uncover the threads that connect the past to the present, creating experiences that will stay with you long after you've left. Each castle, each stone, has a story to tell, and Cardigan Bay is the perfect place to listen.

More Historic Gems

Strata Florida Abbey

Tucked away in the scenic heart of Cardiganshire, Strata Florida Abbey is a site of profound historical and spiritual significance. This Cistercian abbey, founded in the 12th century, is a testament to the enduring presence of religion and culture in the region.

As you approach Strata Florida Abbey, the first thing that strikes you is its remote and tranquil setting. Surrounded by rolling green hills, this abbey was deliberately established in a secluded location, where monks could dedicate themselves to a life of prayer and contemplation.

The name "Strata Florida" itself translates to "the Vale of Flowers," and when you visit during the right season, you'll understand why. Wildflowers carpet the abbey's grounds, adding a burst of color to this serene place.

Walking through the abbey's ruins, you'll find yourself transported to a time when monks chanted their daily prayers in the stillness of the cloisters. The abbey's church, with its grand arches and intricate stone carvings, is a testament to the skill of the craftsmen who built it.

Strata Florida Abbey has played a pivotal role in Welsh history. It was not only a center of religious devotion but also a place of learning and culture. Its library once held priceless manuscripts, and it was a gathering place for poets, bards, and scholars, contributing to the rich tapestry of Welsh heritage.

Today, Strata Florida Abbey stands as a hauntingly beautiful testament to the passage of time. Its history is etched in every weathered stone, and the sense of peace that pervades the site is palpable. It's a place to reflect on the centuries that have come and gone and to appreciate the enduring legacy of the people who shaped Cardigan Bay's history.

Pentre Ifan

Venture further into the Cardigan Bay region, and you'll encounter Pentre Ifan, a prehistoric marvel that predates even the ancient castles and abbeys. Pentre Ifan is a Neolithic burial chamber and one of the most iconic megalithic sites in Wales.

This ancient monument is shrouded in mystery. It consists of a massive capstone balanced atop three upright stones, creating a portal-like structure. The purpose of Pentre Ifan remains a subject of debate among archaeologists and historians, adding to its allure.

As you stand before Pentre Ifan, you can't help but be struck by the sheer scale of the stones and the precision with which they were arranged. It's a testament to the engineering prowess of the Neolithic people who built it over 5,000 years ago.

Pentre Ifan's location is equally impressive, set against a backdrop of rolling hills and lush countryside. It's a place where you can connect with the ancient past and ponder the mysteries of our ancestors.

Visiting this historic gem is a humbling experience, reminding us of the enduring human quest to leave our mark on the landscape and to seek understanding in the mysteries of life and death.

Cardigan Bay's historic attractions, from its medieval castles to its ancient megaliths, offer a profound connection to the past. Each site has its own unique story to tell, and exploring them is like turning the pages of a history book, revealing the layers of time that have shaped this extraordinary region.

Museums and Heritage Centers

Cardigan Bay's museums and heritage centers are windows into the past, offering a glimpse into the traditions, industries, and lives of those who have called this region home for generations. Whether you're a history enthusiast or simply curious about the area's heritage, these institutions are well worth a visit.

Cardigan Heritage Center

The Cardigan Heritage Center stands as a beacon of the region's history, providing an immersive experience that will transport you back in time. Located in the heart of Cardigan town, this center is a must-visit for anyone looking to uncover the layers of Cardigan's past.

As you step inside, you'll be greeted by informative exhibits that trace the town's evolution, from its early days as a bustling port to its present-day charm. You'll gain insight into the maritime heritage that once thrived here, with displays of ship models, navigational instruments, and artifacts from the seafaring days.

The center also shines a light on Cardigan's rich Welsh culture. You'll find displays dedicated to the Welsh language, traditional clothing, and the local Eisteddfod festival, which celebrates the arts, music, and literature of Wales. It's an opportunity to immerse yourself in the vibrant traditions that continue to shape the region's identity.

One of the center's standout features is its collection of local tales and legends. These stories are woven into the very fabric of Cardigan Bay, and the center's staff are excellent storytellers who bring these legends to life, captivating you with tales of pirates, sea monsters, and heroic deeds.

For those with an interest in genealogy, the Cardigan Heritage Center is a valuable resource. The staff can assist you in tracing your Welsh ancestry, making it possible to connect with your roots and gain a deeper understanding of your family history.

As you explore this immersive heritage center, you'll find that it's not just a place to learn about the past—it's a place to experience it. The Cardigan Heritage Center hosts workshops, events, and demonstrations that allow you to engage with historical crafts and practices. You might try your hand at traditional Welsh knitting or watch a blacksmith forge in action.

Before you leave, be sure to visit the center's gift shop, where you can find unique souvenirs and locally crafted goods. It's the perfect way to take a piece of Cardigan's history home with you.

Welsh Coastal Heritage Museum

As you explore Cardigan Bay, you'll soon discover that its allure extends beyond its natural landscapes and into its rich cultural heritage. Nestled along the coast, you'll find the Welsh Coastal Heritage Museum, a place that encapsulates the essence of this region's maritime history.

Welsh Coastal Heritage Museum

Welsh Coastal Heritage Museum is a hidden gem that beckons to be explored. It's more than just a museum; it's a window into Cardigan Bay's seafaring past. Here, you can immerse yourself in the maritime history that has shaped the lives of the coastal communities for generations.

Cardigan Bay's Maritime Heritage

The museum is a testament to the strong connection that Cardigan Bay has with the sea. As you step through its doors, you'll be greeted by a world of artifacts, exhibits, and stories that highlight the importance of the sea to the people of this region. From fishing to shipbuilding, the museum offers a comprehensive overview of the maritime traditions that have thrived along the coast.

Exhibits that Come to Life

What sets the Welsh Coastal Heritage Museum apart is its ability to make history come alive. The exhibits are not just static displays but dynamic experiences that engage your senses. You'll find yourself transported back in time as you step onto the meticulously recreated decks of historic ships, hear the tales of sailors, and witness the craftsmanship that went into building vessels that sailed Cardigan Bay's waters.

Maritime Artifacts and Treasures

The museum's collection of maritime artifacts is nothing short of remarkable. From navigational instruments that guided sailors through treacherous waters to intricately carved figureheads that once adorned proud ships, each item tells a story of adventure, hardship, and perseverance. It's a tangible connection to the seafaring souls who called Cardigan Bay home.

Interactive Learning for All Ages

The Welsh Coastal Heritage Museum caters to visitors of all ages. Whether you're a history enthusiast, a curious child, or a seasoned traveler, there's something here for everyone. Interactive exhibits allow you to try your hand at tying knots, handling nautical tools, or even steering a virtual ship. It's a place where learning is fun and hands-on.

Connecting with the Community

One of the most compelling aspects of the museum is its deep connection to the local community. The passionate volunteers and guides who share their knowledge and stories are the heart and soul of this institution. You'll find that conversations with them provide valuable insights into the past and present of Cardigan Bay.

Preserving a Legacy for the Future

The Welsh Coastal Heritage Museum is not just about looking back; it's about preserving the legacy of Cardigan Bay's maritime history for future generations. The museum's commitment to conservation and education ensures that the stories of the sea continue to inspire and inform, making it an essential stop for anyone looking to understand the essence of this region.

Cultural Insights

As you continue your exploration of Cardigan Bay, it's not just the breathtaking landscapes and historical landmarks that will capture your heart; it's also the rich tapestry of culture that defines this region. Cardigan Bay isn't merely a place to visit; it's an opportunity to immerse yourself in the vibrant traditions, art, and lifestyle of its people.

Language and Tradition

Welsh, known as "Cymraeg," is the native language of Wales and holds a special place in the hearts of the people of Cardigan Bay. While English is widely spoken, you'll often hear Welsh spoken in local communities. Even if you're not fluent, learning a few basic Welsh phrases can be a wonderful way to connect with the locals and demonstrate your respect for their culture.

Traditional music and dance are also integral to Cardigan Bay's cultural identity. You might find yourself tapping your feet to the lively tunes of folk music or witnessing a mesmerizing Welsh clog dance performance at a local festival. The rhythm of the region is deeply tied to its traditions.

Festivals and Celebrations

Cardigan Bay comes alive with a myriad of festivals and celebrations throughout the year. One of the most anticipated events is the National Eisteddfod, a Welsh cultural festival that showcases the best in music, poetry, and performance. It's a fantastic opportunity to witness the depth of Welsh artistic talent.

Additionally, don't miss out on local food festivals, where you can savor traditional Welsh delicacies and locally sourced dishes. These gatherings provide a chance to not only indulge in mouthwatering cuisine but also engage with the warmth and hospitality of the locals.

Art and Craftsmanship

The artistic spirit thrives in Cardigan Bay, with a thriving community of painters, sculptors, and craftsmen. The region's stunning landscapes often serve as inspiration for their work. You'll find galleries and workshops where you can admire and even purchase unique pieces of art that capture the essence of this coastal paradise.

Historical Landmarks and Museums

Cardigan Bay is home to several museums and historical landmarks that offer valuable insights into the culture and heritage of the region. Among them is the Cardigan Castle, a beautifully restored fortress that tells the story of centuries of Welsh history. The castle often hosts cultural events and performances, providing a dynamic experience for visitors.

Local Cuisine

No exploration of Cardigan Bay's culture is complete without indulging in its delectable cuisine. Seafood lovers will be in heaven, with fresh catches from the bay transformed into mouthwatering dishes at local restaurants. You must try the famous Cardigan Bay crab and other seafood specialties. And if you're feeling adventurous, sample traditional Welsh dishes like cawl (a hearty soup) or bara brith (a spiced fruitcake).

Community and Hospitality

Above all, what sets Cardigan Bay apart is the warmth and friendliness of its people. The sense of community here is palpable, and you'll often find locals eager to share stories, traditions, and recommendations with you. Don't be shy; strike up a conversation with a shopkeeper, attend a community event, or join a local gathering to experience the true essence of Cardigan Bay's culture.

In conclusion, the region's castles and historic sites, including the magnificent Cardigan Castle and the picturesque Cilgerran Castle, stand as timeless testaments to Wales' rich history. These ancient fortresses transport you to a bygone era, offering a glimpse into the stories of knights, battles, and the enduring spirit of the land.

Moreover, Cardigan Bay's museums and heritage centers, such as the Cardigan Heritage Center and the Welsh Coastal Heritage Museum, serve as educational beacons, illuminating the region's heritage and maritime history. They are windows into the lives of those who have shaped this coastal paradise.

Beyond the tangible history, Cardigan Bay reveals its vibrant soul through cultural insights. From the melodious Welsh language and traditional arts to the warmth of its festivals and the delectable local cuisine, the culture here is both enriching and inviting.

In your exploration of Cardigan Bay, you'll not only witness its castles, historic sites, museums, and cultural gems but also become a part of the timeless tapestry that makes this region a truly unforgettable destination. It's a place where the echoes of the past resonate harmoniously with the present, inviting you to immerse yourself in its captivating stories and embrace the heartwarming spirit of its people.

Dining and Culinary Delights

When you embark on a journey to Cardigan Bay, you're not just treating yourself to breathtaking natural beauty, but also to a delectable culinary experience. This guide will take you on a gastronomic journey through Cardigan Bay, exploring the local cuisine and traditional Welsh dishes that will tantalize your taste buds. So, let's dive into the world of flavors that await you in this stunning region.

Local Cuisine

Cardigan Bay is not only known for its stunning landscapes but also for its rich culinary heritage. The region offers a diverse range of dishes that are sure to please even the most discerning palates. When you visit Cardigan Bay, you'll have the opportunity to savor some of the finest local cuisine that Wales has to offer.

Traditional Welsh Dishes

Cawl - The Heartwarming Broth: Start your culinary journey with a bowl of Cawl, a traditional Welsh soup that warms the soul. This hearty broth is typically made with lamb or beef, potatoes, carrots, and leeks. It's the perfect comfort food after a day of exploring the coastal towns and national parks of Cardigan Bay. You can enjoy a steaming bowl of Cawl at local restaurants for around $10.

Welsh Rarebit - A Cheesy Delight: If you're a cheese lover, Welsh Rarebit is a must-try. It's a simple yet flavorful dish made with a savory cheese sauce served over toasted bread. The combination of sharp cheddar cheese, mustard, and ale creates a deliciously rich topping. A serving of Welsh Rarebit will cost you around $8.

Bara Brith - A Sweet Treat: For dessert, indulge in Bara Brith, a traditional Welsh fruitcake. It's made with dried fruits soaked in tea and mixed with spices, brown sugar, and self-raising flour. Slices of Bara Brith are often served with butter, and you can enjoy this delightful treat for around $5.

Laverbread - A Seaside Specialty: Laverbread is a unique dish made from edible seaweed found along the Cardigan Bay coastline. It's typically served as a side dish and is known for its distinct flavor. You can try Laverbread at local restaurants for approximately $6.

Welsh Cakes - A Sweet Delicacy: Don't leave Cardigan Bay without trying Welsh Cakes. These sweet, griddled cakes are studded with currants or raisins and lightly dusted with sugar. They're perfect for a quick snack or dessert and cost around $4 for a batch.

Welsh Lamb - A Culinary Gem: Cardigan Bay is renowned for its high-quality Welsh lamb. You'll find it featured in various dishes across the region. Whether it's a succulent lamb roast or a savory lamb stew, the tender meat is a culinary gem worth savoring. Prices for lamb dishes vary depending on the restaurant but typically range from $15 to $25.

Seafood Extravaganza - Fresh from the Bay: Being a coastal region, Cardigan Bay offers an array of fresh seafood options. From local catches of fish and shellfish to crab and lobster, seafood lovers will be in paradise. Prices for seafood dishes can vary but generally range from $15 to $30, depending on your choice.

Pies and Pastries - Savory Delights: Keep an eye out for savory pies and pastries filled with delicious ingredients like minced meat, vegetables, and seasonings. These hearty dishes are perfect for a quick lunch and typically cost around $10.

Cardigan Bay's culinary scene is a reflection of its diverse culture and history. Whether you're a foodie or simply seeking authentic Welsh flavors, the region's restaurants, pubs, and cafes have something to offer every palate.

Seafood Specialties

Cawl: Let's start with one of Wales' iconic dishes, Cawl. This hearty soup is a delightful blend of meat (often lamb or beef), potatoes, leeks, carrots, and swedes, seasoned with herbs. It's a comforting dish, perfect for warming up after a day of exploring. You can typically find a bowl of Cawl in local restaurants for around $10 to $15.

Welsh Rarebit: This classic Welsh dish is essentially a savory cheese toast. A rich and creamy cheese sauce, often made with local Welsh cheese like Caerphilly or cheddar, is spread over toasted bread. Sometimes, a bit of mustard and Worcestershire sauce are added for extra flavor. You can enjoy a plate of Welsh Rarebit for approximately $8 to $12.

Laverbread: For a taste of the sea, try Laverbread. It's made from seaweed (laver), which is washed, boiled, and then minced to create a unique paste. It's often served as a side dish or as part of a traditional Welsh breakfast. A serving of Laverbread usually costs around $5 to $8.

Cockles and Laverbread: Combining the flavors of the sea, this dish features cockles (small edible clams) and Laverbread. It's a delightful seafood pairing that you can savor for about $10 to $15.

Fish and Chips: While not exclusive to Wales, you'll find excellent fish and chips throughout Cardigan Bay. Freshly caught fish, often cod or haddock, is battered and fried to perfection. Served with chunky chips and mushy peas, it's a satisfying meal that typically costs around $12 to $18.

Seafood Platter: If you're a seafood enthusiast, indulge in a seafood platter. These platters feature a variety of fresh catches from Cardigan Bay, including crab, lobster, mussels, and prawns. Prices for seafood platters can vary depending on the selection but usually start at $30 and can go up from there.

Pembrokeshire Lobster: Pembrokeshire, part of the Cardigan Bay region, is renowned for its succulent lobsters. Grilled or boiled, Pembrokeshire lobster is a delicacy worth trying. Prices can range from $25 to $40 or more, depending on the size and preparation.

Cardigan Bay Oysters: If you're a fan of oysters, you're in for a treat. Cardigan Bay is home to some of the finest oysters in Wales. Served fresh and typically with a squeeze of lemon, a half-dozen oysters can cost around $12 to $18.

Welsh Cakes: For dessert or a sweet treat, don't miss out on Welsh cakes. These delightful griddle cakes are made with butter, sugar, and currants, resulting in a slightly sweet and buttery flavor. A bag of Welsh cakes is a steal at about $5 to $8.

Bara Brith: Lastly, satisfy your sweet tooth with Bara Brith. This traditional Welsh fruitcake is infused with tea and dried fruits, creating a moist and flavorful dessert. A slice of Bara Brith usually costs around $4 to $6.

Local Restaurants and Cafés

Cardigan boasts a range of local restaurants and cafés that offer a delightful culinary experience. Here, we'll take you on a gastronomic tour of some of the must-visit establishments.

Gwesty'r Emlyn Hotel Restaurant

Located in the heart of Cardigan town, Gwesty'r Emlyn Hotel Restaurant is a culinary gem that offers a fine dining experience. The menu here showcases the best of Welsh cuisine, with an emphasis on locally sourced ingredients. As you dine here, you'll savor the rich flavors of dishes like Cawl, a traditional Welsh soup, and fresh seafood caught in Cardigan Bay itself. The cozy atmosphere and friendly service make it a perfect spot for a romantic dinner or special occasion.

Crwst

If you're looking for a charming café to enjoy a cup of coffee and delicious pastries, Crwst is the place to be. Situated in the town center, Crwst is a haven for foodies and coffee lovers alike. Their artisanal pastries, crafted with love and precision, are simply divine. Pair your latte with a warm, flaky croissant, or indulge in one of their delectable cakes. The cozy interior and welcoming staff create a warm and inviting atmosphere that's perfect for a leisurely morning or afternoon.

Pizzatipi

For those craving a taste of Italy in the heart of Cardigan, Pizzatipi is the go-to spot. This quirky pizzeria is tucked away along the river Teifi, offering not only scrumptious wood-fired pizzas but also a unique and rustic ambiance. The dough is made fresh daily, and the toppings include a variety of locally sourced and seasonal ingredients. With picnic tables set under the canopy of trees and the gentle sound of the river, it's a fantastic place to enjoy a casual meal with friends or family.

Bara Menyn Bakehouse and Café

If you're a fan of artisan bread and wholesome, homemade dishes, Bara Menyn Bakehouse and Café will be your haven. This cozy café is a haven for lovers of freshly baked bread, pastries, and hearty lunches. From their sourdough loaves to their quiches and soups, everything here is made with a commitment to quality and taste. The café's rustic charm and friendly staff make it a favorite among locals and visitors alike.

The Ship Inn

For a taste of Cardigan's maritime history and a hearty pub meal, The Ship Inn is the place to visit. This historic pub, overlooking the river, has been serving patrons for centuries. You can savor traditional pub fare here, such as fish and chips, alongside a selection of local ales and ciders. The cozy interior is adorned with nautical decor, adding to the charm of this establishment. It's a welcoming spot for both lunch and dinner.

Fforest Pizza Tipi

For a truly unique dining experience, head to Fforest Pizza Tipi, located within the Fforest campsite. This enchanting tipi, nestled in a forest clearing, offers wood-fired pizzas that are nothing short of extraordinary. The ingredients used are locally sourced and often organic, resulting in deliciously fresh and vibrant flavors. Dining here is a communal affair, as you share long wooden tables with fellow travelers. The crackling fire in the center of the tipi adds to the magical atmosphere, making it a memorable spot for both couples and families.

Pendre Art

Pendre Art is a charming little café that combines art with cuisine. Located in the town of Cardigan, this establishment not only serves delectable food but also showcases the work of local artists. The menu features an array of sandwiches, quiches, and cakes, all prepared with an artistic touch. It's a wonderful place to enjoy a light lunch while admiring the talent of the local creative community.

Tŷ Cegin

Tŷ Cegin is a hidden gem tucked away in the Teifi Valley. This family-run café and bakery is known for its warm hospitality and mouthwatering cakes. Their scones, in particular, are legendary, served with clotted cream and homemade jam. Whether you're stopping by for breakfast or afternoon tea, you'll be greeted with a smile and the tempting aroma of freshly baked treats.

The Castle Inn

If you're in the mood for a traditional pub experience with a hearty meal, The Castle Inn is the place to be. Located near Cardigan Castle, this historic pub exudes character and charm. The menu includes classic pub dishes, such as steak and ale pie, along with a selection of local ales and ciders. The welcoming atmosphere and friendly locals make it a great spot to immerse yourself in the community's culture while enjoying a satisfying meal.

The Mwldan

For a fusion of culture, cinema, and cuisine, The Mwldan is a cultural hub in Cardigan. This venue hosts not only live performances and film screenings but also features a delightful café. The menu offers a diverse range of options, from light bites to full meals. Their commitment to using local ingredients ensures that you'll enjoy a fresh and flavorful dining experience. After your meal, you can catch a film or enjoy a live performance, making it a perfect evening outing.

Thus, the local restaurants and cafes in Cardigan offer a delightful blend of flavors, settings, and experiences.

Chapter 8

Practical Information

Useful Phrases Welsh is a beautiful language that adds a unique cultural dimension to your experience in Cardigan Bay. While English is widely spoken, knowing a few Welsh phrases can enhance your interactions and show respect for the local culture.

Common Welsh Phrases

- Bore da (bore deh) - Good morning.
- Prynhawn da (prin-houn da) - Good afternoon.
- Noswaith dda (nos-waith tha) - Good evening.
- Nos da (nos da) - Good night.
- Hwyl fawr (hoo-eel vaur) - Goodbye.
- Croeso (kroy-so) - Welcome.
- "Diolch" (pronounced: dee-olch) - Thank you.
- "Diolch yn fawr" (pronounced: dee-olch un vaur) - Thank you very much.
- "Os gwelwch yn dda" (pronounced: os gwel-ookh un dha) - Please.
- "Sut mae?" (pronounced: sit my) - How are you?
- "Da iawn, diolch" (pronounced: da yow-n, dee-olch) - I'm well, thank you.
- "Ble mae'r toiled?" (pronounced: bleh myr toy-led) - Where is the toilet?

- "Hoffwn i brynu hyn" (pronounced: hof-win ee bru-ni hun) - I would like to buy this.
- "Beth ydy hwn?" (pronounced: beth uhd-ee hoon) - What is this?
- "Ga i fwydlen, os gwelwch yn dda?" (pronounced: ga ee mwoy-dlen, os gwel-ookh un dha) - May I have a menu, please?
- "Dw i'n hoffi hyn" (pronounced: doo een hof-ee hun) - I like this.
- "Dw i ddim yn hoffi hyn" (pronounced: doo ee deem un hof-ee hun) - I don't like this.
- "Cynnes iawn" (pronounced: kun-ess ee-oun) - Very warm (weather).
- "Mae'n bwrw glaw" (pronounced: myn boor-oo glou) - It's raining.
- "Tywydd braf heddiw" (pronounced: tuh-oo-ith brahf heh-thiw) - Nice weather today.
- "Gwyntog" (pronounced: goo-in-tog) - Windy.
- "Hapus" (pronounced: hap-iss) - Happy.
- "Llygoden fach" (pronounced: luh-god-en vahkh) - Mouse.
- "Cath" (pronounced: kath) - Cat.
- "Ci" (pronounced: kee) - Dog.
- "Esgid" (pronounced: ess-geed) - Shoe.
- "Bag" (pronounced: bag) - Bag.
- "Cerdded" (pronounced: ker-thed) - Walking.
- "Siop" (pronounced: shop) - Shop.
- "Arian" (pronounced: ah-ree-an) - Money.
- "Pwy ydych chi?" (pronounced: pwee uhd-ikh khi) - Who are you?
- "Cyfarchion" (pronounced: kuh-var-khion) - Greetings.
- "Pethau i wneud" (pronounced: peh-thai ee oo-noid) - Things to do.
- "Llyfrgell" (pronounced: luhr-ghel) - Library.
- "Ffôn" (pronounced: fon) - Phone.

- "Tren" (pronounced: tren) - Train.
- "Bws" (pronounced: boos) - Bus.
- "Trên hwn i Aberystwyth, os gwelwch yn dda" (pronounced: tren hoon ee Aber-ist-with, os gwel-ookh un dha) - This train to Aberystwyth, please.
- "Dwi'n hoffi cerdded" (pronounced: doo-een hof-ee ker-thed) - I like walking.
- "Dw i'n dysgu Cymraeg" (pronounced: doo-een dus-gee kum-ryeig) - I am learning Welsh.
- "Dw i wedi blino" (pronounced: doo-een wed-ee bleen-o) - I am tired.
- "Dw i'n hoffi'r traeth" (pronounced: doo-een hof-ee-ur trayth) - I like the beach.
- "Dw i'n hoffi bwyta" (pronounced: doo-een hof-ee boo-ee-ta) - I like eating.
- "Dw i'n hoffi'r bwyd" (pronounced: doo-een hof-ee-ur boo-id) - I like the food.
- "Yr haul yn disgleirio" (pronounced: ur hahl un dis-glay-ree-o) - The sun is shining.
- "Yr awyr yn las" (pronounced: ur ah-oo-ir un las) - The sky is blue.
- "Mae hi'n bwrw eira" (pronounced: my hi-n boor-oo ay-ra) - It's snowing.
- "Dw i eisiau coffi" (pronounced: doo-een ay-shy-eye kof-ee) - I want coffee.
- "Pwy sy'n canu?" (pronounced: pwee sun ka-nee) - Who is singing?
- "Dw i'n mynd i'r traeth" (pronounced: doo-een muhnd eer trai-th) - I'm going to the beach.
- "Dw i'n hoffi'r cerddoriaeth" (pronounced: doo-een hof-ee-ur ker-thor-ee-ath) - I like the music.

- "Dw i'n hoffi darllen" (pronounced: doo-een hof-ee dar-lehn) - I like reading.
- "Dw i'n hoffi ffilmiau" (pronounced: doo-een hof-ee ffeel-my-eye) - I like movies.
- "Dw i'n hoffi hwylio" (pronounced: doo-een hof-ee hoo-ee-lo) - I like sailing.
- "Dw i'n hoffi nofio" (pronounced: doo-een hof-ee noh-vee-oh) - I like swimming.
- "Dw i'n hoffi cymryd lluniau" (pronounced: doo-een hof-ee kum-ridh llee-nye-eye) - I like taking photos.
- "Dw i'n hoffi'r canolfan siopa" (pronounced: doo-een hof-ee-ur kan-ol-van shop-a) - I like the shopping center.
- "Pwy sy'n rheolwr?" (pronounced: pwee sun rhe-o-loor) - Who is the manager?
- "Dw i'n colli fy nghyfrif" (pronounced: doo-een koh-lee vuh ng-kuh-reev) - I lost my wallet.
- "Faint mae hyn?" (pronounced: faynt my hoon) - How much is this?
- "Dw i'n hoffi cerdded ar y traeth" (pronounced: doo-een hof-ee ker-thed ar ur trayth) - I like walking on the beach.
- "Mae'r tŷ yn hardd" (pronounced: myr tee un har-th) - The house is beautiful.
- "Beth ydych chi'n wneud?" (pronounced: beth uhd-ikh khi-n oo-noid) - What are you doing?
- "Pwy ydych chi'n mynd gyda fi?" (pronounced: pwee uhd-ikh khi-n muhnd guh-da vee) - Who is coming with me?
- "Pryd ydych chi'n mynd?" (pronounced: prid uhd-ikh khi-n muhnd) - When are you going?
- "Ydw, dw i'n hoffi te" (pronounced: ud-oo, doo een hof-ee te) - Yes, I like tea.

- "Nac ydw, dw i ddim yn hoffi coffi" (pronounced: nak ud-oo, doo een deem un hof-ee kof-ee) - No, I don't like coffee.
- "Pwy sy'n perfformio?" (pronounced: pwee sun per-for-mee-o) - Who is performing?
- "Dw i eisiau teisen" (pronounced: doo-een ay-shy-eye tay-sen) - I want cake.
- "Pam?" (pronounced: pam) - Why?
- "Dw i ddim yn gwybod" (pronounced: doo-een deem un goo-ee-bod) - I don't know.
- "Dw i eisiau mynd i'r parc" (pronounced: doo-een ay-shy-eye muhnd eer park) - I want to go to the park.
- "Pa mor bell?" (pronounced: pa mor bel) - How far?
- "Pwy yw'r prifathro?" (pronounced: pwee-uh-oo prif-ath-ro) - Who is the headmaster?
- "Dw i'n mynd i'r sinema heno" (pronounced: doo-een muhnd eer sin-eh-ma heh-no) - I'm going to the cinema tonight.
- "Dw i eisiau peint" (pronounced: doo-een ay-shy-eye paint) - I want a pint.
- "Mae'r blodau yn hardd" (pronounced: myr blod-eye un har-th) - The flowers are beautiful.
- "Dw i'n hoffi darllen llyfrau" (pronounced: doo-een hof-ee dar-lehn llee-vry) - I like reading books.
- "Pam ydych chi'n chwerthin?" (pronounced: pam uhd-ikh khi-n kwer-thin) - Why are you laughing?
- "Beth sy'n digwydd?" (pronounced: beth sun dig-oo-ith) - What's happening?
- "Dw i'n mynd i'r parti" (pronounced: doo-een muhnd eer par-tee) - I'm going to the party.
- "Pryd fyddwch chi'n dod yn ôl?" (pronounced: prid vu-dookh khi-n dod un oh-l) - When will you come back?

- "Dw i eisiau teisen ffrwythau" (pronounced: doo-een ay-shy-eye tay-sen fur-oo-eye) - I want fruit cake.
- "Dw i eisiau mynd i'r môr" (pronounced: doo-een ay-shy-eye muhnd eer mohr) - I want to go to the sea.
- "Sut ydych chi'n teimlo?" (pronounced: sit uhd-ikh khi-n tame-lo) - How do you feel?
- "Dw i'n hoffi cerdded gyda fy nheulu" (pronounced: doo-een hof-ee ker-thed guh-da vuh ng-hail-ee) - I like walking with my family.
- "Hwyl fawr am nawr" (pronounced: hoo-eel vaur am naor) - Goodbye for now.
- "Dw i'n mwynhau'r awyr agored" (pronounced: doo-een mwin-hai-r ah-oo-ir ah-gor-ed) - I enjoy the outdoors.
- "Ydw, dw i'n hoffi mwynhau'r awyr agored" (pronounced: ud-oo, doo-een hof-ee mwin-hai-r ah-oo-ir ah-gor-ed) - Yes, I like to enjoy the outdoors.
- "Nac ydw, dw i ddim yn hoffi mwynhau'r awyr agored" (pronounced: nak ud-oo, doo-een deem un hof-ee mwin-hai-r ah-oo-ir ah-gor-ed) - No, I don't like to enjoy the outdoors.
- "Beth yw dy hoff bryd?" (pronounced: beth-uh-oo duh hof bru-id) - What is your favorite meal?
- "Dw i'n mwynhau canu a chwarae gitâr" (pronounced: doo-een mwin-hai kah-nee ah khwah-rye gee-tar) - I enjoy singing and playing guitar.
- "Dw i'n mwynhau teithio ac archwilio" (pronounced: doo-een mwin-hai tay-thee-o ahk ar-khwee-lee-o) - I enjoy traveling and exploring.
- "Dw i'n mwynhau gwylio ffilmiau" (pronounced: doo-ccn mwin-hai goo-ee-lee-o ffeel-my-eye) - I enjoy watching movies.

- "Sut wyt ti'n teimlo am fwyd Cymraeg?" (pronounced: sit wit tee-n tame-lo am booid kum-rayg) - How do you feel about Welsh food?
- "Dw i'n hoffi clywed cerddoriaeth traddodiadol Cymru" (pronounced: doo-een hof-ee kleh-wed ker-thor-ee-ath trah-dod-ee-odd-ol kum-ree) - I like listening to traditional Welsh music.
- "Dw i'n mwynhau ymweld â mannau hanesyddol" (pronounced: doo-een mwin-hai um-weld ah man-eye han-ess-uh-thol) - I enjoy visiting historical places.
- "Dw i'n mwynhau gwylio'r gêm rygbi" (pronounced: doo-een mwin-hai goo-ee-lee-or game rug-bee) - I enjoy watching rugby games.
- "Dw i'n mwynhau chwarae pel-droed" (pronounced: doo-een mwin-hai khwah-rye pel-droyd) - I enjoy playing football (soccer).
- "Dw i'n hoffi pethau sy'n gyfrifol" (pronounced: doo-een hof-ee peh-thai sun guh-free-vol) - I like responsible things.
- "Pam wyt ti'n mwynhau deithio?" (pronounced: pam wit tee-n mwin-hai day-thee-o) - Why do you enjoy traveling?
- "Beth wyt ti'n mwynhau yfed?" (pronounced: beth wit tee-n mwin-hai uh-ved) - What do you enjoy drinking?
- "Dw i'n hoffi chwarae chwaraeon" (pronounced: doo-een hof-ee khwah-rye khwah-ray-on) - I like playing sports.
- "Dw i'n hoffi mynd i'r ffair" (pronounced: doo-een hof-ee muhnd eer figh-r) - I like going to the fair.
- "Dw i'n hoffi cerdded ar hyd y traeth" (pronounced: doo-een hof-ee ker-thed ar heed ur trayth) - I like walking along the beach.
- "Beth wyt ti'n mwynhau gwneud gyda dy ffrindiau?" (pronounced: beth wit tee-n mwin-hai goo-noid guh-da duh frin-dee-eye) - What do you enjoy doing with your friends?

- "Pwy yw dy hoff artist?" (pronounced: pwee uh-oo duh hoff artist) - Who is your favorite artist?
- "Beth yw dy hoff fwyd dramor?" (pronounced: beth-uh-oo duh hoff booid tra-mor) - What is your favorite foreign food?
- "Dw i'n hoffi bwyta allan yn ystod y penwythnos" (pronounced: doo-een hof-ee booy-ta al-lan uhn us-tod uh pen-with-nos) - I like eating out during the weekend.
- "Beth wyt ti'n mwynhau gwisgo?" (pronounced: beth wit tee-n mwin-hai goo-ee-sgo) - What do you enjoy wearing?
- "Dw i'n hoffi bod yn y natur" (pronounced: doo-een hof-ee bod uhn uh nat-oor) - I like being in nature.
- "Dw i'n hoffi bod ar y traeth wrth y mor" (pronounced: doo-een hof-ee bod ar ur trayth oo-rth uh mor) - I like being on the beach by the sea.
- "Pwy yw dy hoff awdur?" (pronounced: pwee uh-oo duh hoff ow-dur) - Who is your favorite author?
- "Dw i'n hoffi bwyta allan gyda fy nheulu" (pronounced: doo-een hof-ee booy-ta al-lan guh-da vuh ng-hail-ee) - I like eating out with my family.
- "Dw i'n hoffi treulio amser gyda fy ffrindiau" (pronounced: doo-een hof-ee tray-lee-o am-sair guh-da vuh frin-dee-eye) - I like spending time with my friends.
- "Pwy yw dy hoff athro?" (pronounced: pwee uh-oo duh hoff ath-ro) - Who is your favorite teacher?
- "Dw i'n hoffi chwarae gemau cyfrifiadur" (pronounced: doo-een hof-ee khwah-rye geh-mai ku-vri-vad-ur) - I like playing computer games.
- "Dw i'n hoffi canu yn y stiwdio" (pronounced: doo-een hof-ee ka-nee un uh stee-ood-io) - I like singing in the studio.
- "Pwy yw dy hoff fand?" (pronounced: pwee uh-oo duh hoff mand) - Who is your favorite band?

- "Dw i'n hoffi mwynhau'r awyr iach" (pronounced: doo-een hof-ee mwin-hai-ur ah-oo-ir yaakh) - I like enjoying the fresh air.
- "Beth wyt ti'n mwynhau neud pan mae hi'n bwrw eira?" (pronounced: beth wit tee-n mwin-hai nide pan my hi-n boor-oo ay-ra) - What do you enjoy doing when it's snowing?
- "Dw i'n hoffi casglu perlysiau" (pronounced: doo-een hof-ee kas-glee per-lee-sia) - I like collecting pearls.
- "Dw i'n hoffi casglu stamps" (pronounced: doo-een hof-ee kas-glee stamps) - I like collecting stamps.
- "Beth wyt ti'n hoffi neud ar y penwythnos?" (pronounced: beth wit tee-n hof-ee nide ar uh pen-with-nos) - What do you like to do on the weekends?
- "Dw i'n hoffi mwynhau'r haul" (pronounced: doo-een hof-ee mwin-hai-ur heye) - I like enjoying the sun.
- "Pwy yw dy hoff fasnachwr?" (pronounced: pwee uh-oo duh hoff vas-nach-oor) - Who is your favorite merchant?
- "Beth wyt ti'n hoffi neud pan mae hi'n bwrw glaw yn dwym?" (pronounced: beth wit tee-n hof-ee nide pan my hi-n boor-oo glaw un dweem) - What do you like to do when it's warm and raining?
- "Dw i'n hoffi casglu peintiadau" (pronounced: doo-een hof-ee kas-glee paint-ya-dye) - I like collecting paintings.
- "Dw i'n hoffi casglu atgofion" (pronounced: doo-een hof-ee kas-glee at-gov-yon) - I like collecting memories.
- "Pwy yw dy hoff gyfarwyddwr?" (pronounced: pwee uh-oo duh hoff guh-var-oo-ith-oor) - Who is your favorite director?
- "Dw i'n hoffi casglu chwedlau" (pronounced: doo-een hof-ee kas-gloo kweh-dlai) - I like collecting legends.
- "Pwy yw dy hoff awyrennwr?" (pronounced: pwee uh-oo duh hoff ah-wi-ren-oor) - Who is your favorite pilot?

- "Dw i'n hoffi casglu llyfrau" (pronounced: doo-een hof-ee kas-glee llee-vray) - I like collecting books.
- "Pwy yw dy hoff beiriant?" (pronounced: pwee uh-oo duh hoff bay-ree-ant) - Who is your favorite scientist?
- "Dw i'n hoffi casglu chyffro" (pronounced: doo-een hof-ee kas-gloo khuhf-ro) - I like collecting excitement.
- "Beth wyt ti'n mwynhau darllen pan mae hi'n dawel?" (pronounced: beth wit tee-n mwin-hai dar-lehn pan my hi-n dah-wel) - What do you enjoy reading when it's quiet?
- "Pwy yw dy hoff lyfrgellydd?" (pronounced: pwee uh-oo duh hoff luhr-ghel-uth) - Who is your favorite librarian?
- "Beth wyt ti'n hoffi neud pan mae hi'n bwrw eira?" (pronounced: beth wit tee-n hof-ee goo-noid pan my hi-n boor-oo ay-ra) - What do you like to do when it's snowing?
- "Dw i'n hoffi casglu cofion" (pronounced: doo-een hof-ee kas-gloo kov-yon) - I like collecting memories.
- "Pwy yw dy hoff gyfarwyddwr?" (pronounced: pwee uh-oo duh hoff guh-var-oo-ith-oor) - Who is your favorite director?
- "Dw i'n hoffi casglu chwedlau rhyfedd" (pronounced: doo-een hof-ee kas-gloo khwehd-lai roo-ved) - I like collecting strange tales.
- "Pwy yw dy hoff beiriant?" (pronounced: pwee uh-oo duh hoff bay-ree-ant) - Who is your favorite scientist?
- "Dw i'n hoffi casglu arwyr" (pronounced: doo-een hof-ee kas-glee ar-weer) - I like collecting heroes.
- "Pwy yw dy hoff lyfrgellydd?" (pronounced: pwee uh-oo duh hoff luhr-ghel-uth) - Who is your favorite librarian?
- "Beth wyt ti'n hoffi neud pan mae hi'n bwrw eira?" (pronounced: beth wit tee-n hof-ee goo-noid pan my hi-n boor-oo ay-ra) - What do you like to do when it's snowing?

- "Dw i'n hoffi casglu cerddoriaeth draddodiadol" (pronounced: doo-een hof-ee kas-gloo ker-thor-ee-ath thrah-dod-ee-odd-ol) - I like collecting traditional music.
- "Pwy yw dy hoff gyfarwyddwr?" (pronounced: pwee uh-oo duh hoff guh-var-oo-ith-oor) - Who is your favorite director?
- "Dw i'n hoffi casglu chwedlau dychanol" (pronounced: doo-een hof-ee kas-gloo khwehd-lai duh-kha-nol) - I like collecting supernatural tales.
- "Pwy yw dy hoff beiriant?" (pronounced: pwee uh-oo duh hoff bay-ree-ant) - Who is your favorite scientist?
- "Dw i'n hoffi casglu chwedlau gwrthrychol" (pronounced: doo-een hof-ee kas-gloo khwehd-lai goo-rrh-uh-khol) - I like collecting collectible tales.
- "Pwy yw dy hoff lyfrgellydd?" (pronounced: pwee uh-oo duh hoff luhr-ghel-uth) - Who is your favorite librarian?
- "Beth wyt ti'n hoffi neud pan mae hi'n bwrw eira?" (pronounced: beth wit tee-n hof-ee goo-noid pan my hi-n boor-oo ay-ra) - What do you like to do when it's snowing?
- "Dw i'n hoffi casglu cofnodion hanesyddol" (pronounced: doo-een hof-ee kas-gloo kof-noh-dee-on han-ess-uh-thol) - I like collecting historical records.
- "Pwy yw dy hoff gyfarwyddwr?" (pronounced: pwee uh-oo duh hoff guh-var-oo-ith-oor) - Who is your favorite director?
- "Dw i'n hoffi casglu cerddoriaeth byw" (pronounced: doo-een hof-ee kas-gloo ker-thor-ee-ath bii-oo) - I like collecting live music.
- "Beth wyt ti'n mwynhau darllen pan mae hi'n wyntog?" (pronounced: beth wit tee-n mwin-hai dar-lehn pan my hi-n goo-in-tog) - What do you enjoy reading when it's windy?
- "Pwy yw dy hoff beiriant?" (pronounced: pwee uh-oo duh hoff bay-ree-ant) - Who is your favorite scientist?

- "Dw i'n hoffi casglu chwedlau diddorol" (pronounced: doo-een hof-ee kas-gloo khwehd-lai dee-tho-rol) - I like collecting interesting tales.
- "Pwy yw dy hoff lyfrgellydd?" (pronounced: pwee uh-oo duh hoff luhr-ghel-uth) - Who is your favorite librarian?
- "Dw i'n hoffi casglu adnoddau naturiol" (pronounced: doo-een hof-ee kas-gloo ad-noh-thee nahr-oo-yol) - I like collecting natural resources.
- "Pwy yw dy hoff gyfarwyddwr?" (pronounced: pwee uh-oo duh hoff guh-var-oo-ith-oor) - Who is your favorite director?
- "Dw i'n hoffi casglu arteffactau hanesyddol" (pronounced: doo-een hof-ee kas-gloo ar-teh-fakh-tai han-ess-uh-thol) - I like collecting historical artifacts.
- "Pwy yw dy hoff beiriant?" (pronounced: pwee uh-oo duh hoff bay-ree-ant) - Who is your favorite scientist?
- "Dw i'n hoffi casglu arteffactau hynafol" (pronounced: doo-een hof-ee kas-gloo ar-teh-fakh-tai hoo-naf-ol) - I like collecting ancient artifacts.
- "Pwy yw dy hoff lyfrgellydd?" (pronounced: pwee uh-oo duh hoff luhr-ghel-uth) - Who is your favorite librarian?
- "Dw i'n hoffi casglu chwedlau ffantasi" (pronounced: doo-een hof-ee kas-gloo khwehd-lai fan-tah-see) - I like collecting fantasy tales.
- "Pwy yw dy hoff gyfarwyddwr?" (pronounced: pwee uh-oo duh hoff guh-var-oo-ith-oor) - Who is your favorite director?
- "Dw i'n hoffi casglu gemau chwaraeon" (pronounced: doo-een hof-ee kas-gloo geh-mai khwah-rye-on) - I like collecting sports games.
- "Pwy yw dy hoff beiriant?" (pronounced: pwee uh-oo duh hoff bay-ree-ant) - Who is your favorite scientist?

- "Dw i'n hoffi casglu gemau rasio" (pronounced: doo-een hof-ee kas-gloo geh-mai ra-si-oh) - I like collecting racing games.
- "Pwy yw dy hoff lyfrgellydd?" (pronounced: pwee uh-oo duh hoff luhr-ghel-uth) - Who is your favorite librarian?
- "Dw i'n hoffi casglu gemau strategol" (pronounced: doo-een hof-ee kas-gloo geh-mai stra-teh-gol) - I like collecting strategy games.
- "Pwy yw dy hoff gyfarwyddwr?" (pronounced: pwee uh-oo duh hoff guh-var-oo-ith-oor) - Who is your favorite director?
- "Dw i'n hoffi casglu gemau gweithredu" (pronounced: doo-een hof-ee kas-gloo geh-mai gweith-reh-dee) - I like collecting action games.

Now that you have common Welsh phrases with pronunciation patterns, you can use them to enhance your communication and understanding when visiting Cardigan Bay or any other Welsh-speaking area. These phrases cover a wide range of topics, allowing you to engage in conversations, ask questions, and express your preferences while enjoying your time in this beautiful region.

Conclusion

Congratulations! You've journeyed through the pages of this guidebook, uncovering the wonders of Cardigan Bay. Now, as you prepare to embark on your adventure, let's wrap it up with some essential insights to ensure you make the most of your visit to this stunning region.

Highlights Recap

Before you set off on your Cardigan Bay adventure, let's recap some of the highlights you've discovered in this guide:

Beaches: Cardigan Bay boasts a diverse collection of beaches, from the secluded beauty of Mwnt Beach to the family-friendly shores of Poppit Sands and the serene Traeth Penbryn. Each offers a unique experience, so choose the one that resonates with you.

National Parks: Explore the pristine landscapes of Pembrokeshire Coast National Park in the south, with its coastal beauty and hiking trails. To the north, Snowdonia National Park beckons with its towering peaks and charming villages. Nature enthusiasts and hikers will find these parks a paradise.

Coastal Towns: Immerse yourself in the culture and history of coastal towns like Aberystwyth, New Quay, and Aberaeron. From historic libraries to colorful houses, each town has its character waiting to be explored.

Wildlife: Cardigan Bay is home to a vibrant marine ecosystem. Keep an eye out for bottlenose dolphins, harbor porpoises, and seals as they play in the bay's waters. The skies are alive with seabirds, adding to the region's natural beauty.

Exploring Cardigan Bay: Whether you're a hiker, cyclist, or boat enthusiast, there are plenty of activities to keep you engaged. Discover hiking trails that offer panoramic views, cycling routes that wind through picturesque landscapes, and boat tours that bring you closer to marine life.

Planning Your Trip: Don't forget the practicalities. Learn about how to get to Cardigan Bay, find accommodation that suits your style, savor the local cuisine, and pick up some essential travel tips to ensure a smooth journey.

Making the Most of Your Cardigan Bay Adventure

As you prepare to embark on your journey, it's crucial to maximize your experience in Cardigan Bay. Here are some main points to consider:

Timing is Everything: The timing of your visit can greatly impact your experience. If you're a fan of warm weather and beach activities, the summer months of June to August are ideal. Spring and autumn are perfect for hikers, while winter offers a serene atmosphere for relaxation.

Pack Wisely: Depending on the activities you have planned; ensure you pack appropriately. Sunscreen, comfortable hiking shoes, and waterproof gear are valuable companions. Don't forget your camera or binoculars for wildlife spotting.

Engage with the Locals: The warmth and friendliness of the locals in Cardigan Bay are part of what makes this region special. Strike up conversations, ask for recommendations, and embrace the Welsh culture. It's a chance to enrich your experience.

Respect Nature: Cardigan Bay is a protected area, so it's essential to respect the environment. Follow designated trails, dispose of trash responsibly, and maintain a safe distance from wildlife, especially seals and their pups.

Stay Safe: Prioritize safety during your adventure. Check weather forecasts, inform someone of your plans if you're heading into remote areas, and carry essential supplies. Mobile phone signals can be unreliable in some parts of the region, so be prepared.

Try Local Cuisine: Don't miss the opportunity to savor the local cuisine. Welsh dishes like cawl (a hearty soup) and Welsh cakes are must-tries. Explore restaurants, cafes, and markets to taste the flavors of Cardigan Bay.

Highlights Recap

Before we conclude, let's recap some of the must-see highlights that you won't want to miss during your Cardigan Bay adventure:

Dolphin Watching: Join a boat tour to witness the playful bottlenose dolphins leaping in the bay's crystal-clear waters. It's a magical experience that will stay with you forever.

Hiking Trails: Lace up your hiking boots and explore the scenic trails of the national parks. The Pembrokeshire Coast Path and Snowdonia's challenging hikes offer breathtaking views and a deep connection with nature.

Coastal Town Exploration: Stroll through the charming streets of Aberystwyth, New Quay, and Aberaeron. Discover the local history, visit museums, and savor delicious seafood dishes in coastal restaurants.

Sunset Views: Don't forget to catch a Cardigan Bay sunset. Whether you're on the beach, on a clifftop, or in a cozy coastal town, the sunsets here are a mesmerizing blend of colors.

Wildlife Encounters: Keep your eyes peeled for wildlife throughout your journey. Whether it's spotting seals from the shore or seabirds soaring above, Cardigan Bay's wildlife is a constant companion.

In conclusion, Cardigan Bay is a region of unparalleled beauty and diversity, offering something for every traveler. It's a place to reconnect with nature, immerse yourself in Welsh culture, and create lasting memories. As you embark on your adventure, remember to embrace the spirit of exploration, take in the breathtaking scenery, and cherish the unique experiences that Cardigan Bay has to offer. Your journey here promises to be an unforgettable one, filled with discoveries and moments of awe. Safe travels, and may your Cardigan Bay adventure be everything you've imagined and more.

Memories and Recommendations

As your Cardigan Bay adventure draws to a close, it's time to reflect on the memories you've created and offer some valuable recommendations to future travelers. These cherished memories will serve as a reminder of the beauty and wonder you've experienced in this stunning region.

Memories to Treasure

Dolphin Dance: The sight of bottlenose dolphins dancing in the waves is a memory that will forever be etched in your mind. The joy and grace of these creatures as they frolic in the bay's waters are truly enchanting.

Sunset Serenity: The breathtaking sunsets over Cardigan Bay are moments of pure serenity. Whether you watched the sun dip below the horizon from a beach, a clifftop, or a coastal town, the vivid colors and tranquility of those moments are unforgettable.

Nature's Symphony: The sounds of nature surround you in Cardigan Bay. From the soothing rustle of leaves on a coastal hike to the chorus of seabirds overhead, the region's natural symphony provides a sense of peace and harmony.

Coastal Charm: Exploring the coastal towns, with their colorful houses, historic landmarks, and friendly locals, has left you with a deep appreciation for Welsh culture. The warm hospitality and unique character of each town have left an indelible mark.

Wildlife Encounters: Whether you witnessed a seal basking on the rocks or marveled at the intricate flight patterns of seabirds, the wildlife encounters in Cardigan Bay have been both educational and awe-inspiring.

Recommendations for Future Travelers

Plan Ahead: Cardigan Bay offers a wealth of experiences, so plan your trip based on your interests. Whether you're into outdoor adventures, wildlife watching, or cultural exploration, a well-thought-out itinerary will help you make the most of your time here.

Be Nature-Conscious: Remember that Cardigan Bay is a protected area. Respect the environment by following designated trails, picking up litter, and maintaining a safe distance from wildlife.

Your actions can help preserve this natural paradise for generations to come.

Interact with Locals: The locals in Cardigan Bay are friendly and eager to share their knowledge and stories. Engage in conversations, ask for recommendations, and attend local events or festivals to truly immerse yourself in the culture.

Visit in Different Seasons: Consider returning to Cardigan Bay in different seasons to witness its ever-changing beauty. Each season offers a unique perspective, from vibrant summer beach days to tranquil winter retreats.

Sample Local Cuisine: Take the opportunity to savor Welsh dishes in local restaurants and cafes. Try cawl, Welsh cakes, fresh seafood, and other regional specialties to tantalize your taste buds.

Support Conservation: Consider contributing to the conservation efforts in Cardigan Bay. Many organizations work tirelessly to protect the bay's marine life and natural beauty. Your support can make a difference.

Stay Adventurous: Embrace the spirit of exploration during your visit. While this guide has provided a comprehensive overview, there are always hidden gems waiting to be discovered. Be open to unexpected adventures and spontaneous discoveries.

As you prepare to leave Cardigan Bay, remember that the memories you've created and the recommendations you share with fellow travelers will help preserve and celebrate the natural wonders of this remarkable region. Your journey here has been filled with beauty, culture, and unforgettable moments. Carry these experiences with you as you venture onward, and may the spirit of

Cardigan Bay inspire your future travels. Safe journeys, and may your adventures continue to be filled with wonder and discovery.

Cardigan Bay Travel Itinerary

Name:	Duration of Stay:

Hotel Name:	
Arrival Date:	Flight No:

Days	What To Do	Budget
01		
01		
01		
01		
Note		

| Name: | Duration of Stay: |

Hotel Name:	
Arrival Date:	Flight No:

Days	What To Do	Budget
01		
01		
01		
01		
Note		

Name:		**Duration of Stay:**
Hotel Name:		**Flight No:**
Arrival Date:		

Days	What To Do	Budget
01		
01		
01		
01		
Note		

Name:	Duration of Stay:
Hotel Name:	Flight No:
Arrival Date:	

Days	What To Do	Budget
01		
01		
01		
01		
Note		

Name:	Duration of Stay:
Hotel Name:	Flight No:
Arrival Date:	

Days	What To Do	Budget
01		
01		
01		
01		
Note		

| Name: | Duration of Stay: |

| Hotel Name: | |
| Arrival Date: | Flight No: |

Days	What To Do	Budget
01		
01		
01		
01		
Note		

Name:	Duration of Stay:
Hotel Name:	Flight No:
Arrival Date:	

Days	What To Do	Budget
01		
01		
01		
01		
Note		